AF392513

To the reader

Thanks for purchasing this copy, ancient knowledge allows opening the doors to the world of the unknown and the power of the mind.

Omar Hejeile Ch.

AUTHOR
Omar Hejeile Ch.

Wicca editorial, rescue the immeasurable power of the human being and nature; a power that everybody has, feels, prescribes, but few know, through radio shows, encourage without imposing a truth or a concept, so that each one that feel the call from inside, who discovers the magic of dreams, and wants to get the knowledge, thus, the transformation of your life reaches the scepter **of happiness. The old religion has reborn… and is in your hands.**

WICCA
SCHOOL OF MAGIC

The old religion based in the magic knowledge of lost old cultures in time, escaped from the hyperborean world, reborn like the phoenix, the harmony of man with nature. Wicca, word that comes from Wise, Wizard, means *"The job of the wise" "The artisans of wisdom"*.

For millennia of persecution the old documents of the old religion remained hidden waiting for the propitious moment of rebirth, now, Wicca and Ophiuchus, recover some of the old knowledge of the lunar influx, the sun, the great Sabbats, the secret power of enchantments and spells, the art of sorceries, the infinite magic world of plants, the secret of the stars.

More information about WICCA:
www.ofiuco.com
www.radiokronos.com
www.wiccausa.com
www.ophiuchus.us

Wicca

Secrets

Rituals

of

Magic

&

Witchcraft

The future is open to me like the most humble clay to be carved, without being molded, without being but being… the whole possible shapes…

There is a path of a thousand paths which come from me, there is no return, the taken step, buried It is…

INTRODUCTION

The modern human faces unimaginable challenges; the technological society moves forward the conquest of the cosmos, meanwhile the spiritual emptiness and a metaphysic need are growing inside. At the beginning of a new millennium, the trend to return to the ancient knowledge is awakening; it takes place as an alternative to find a comprehensive answer to the human needs. Witchcraft is back, not as a satanic pact, but as the path to harmonize the human being with nature in the search for the occult power of the mind.

Nowadays, far from dogmas and condemnations, the seed of the power of the elements is blooming. The art of harmony with nature brings us ancient recipes of enchantments, sortileges, curses, contributing to get success, attracting progress and breaking free the chains of limitation.

Presidents, managers, business men, housewives, students, workmen, etc., are looking for answers about their future, consulting the different kinds of magical oracles.

The free-spirits are taking new ways towards the future; humanity now is looking for the right direction toward the innerself, discovering the power of the mind.

Giordano Bruno, Johannes Kepler, Galileo Galilei, Nicolaus Copernicus, Socrates, were condemned for finding a light in the darkness of who we are.

The Kybalion says:

"Wherever the master's footprints are, right there,
the ears of that one who is ready to
get his lessons will be wide-open.
Whenever the ear is able to hear, then, the lips
which are supposed to fill it up with
their wisdom will come.
If the possession of wisdom is not complemented
by a manifestation and an expression as in
practicing as in the acting, is equal to burying
precious metals: a vane and useless thing.
The knowledge, just like the fortune,
must be used.
The law of use is universal, and that one who
violates it must suffer for coming into conflicting
against the natural forces."

CHAPTER I

THE PATH OF WITCHCRAFT

"This book has not come to your hands as a coincidence, but as an answer to your thoughts"

Magic is an art, an unknown and limitless world, condemned for millennia to live occult by those which considered the knowledge as a potential enemy against their own interests.

Getting into the magic world is like opening a door towards the imagination, the unknown to nature. Let's start this trip through the adventure of being, picking up the ancient advices and suggestions from the ancestors.

Genesis

Let's travel to the past, in order to find the real meaning of witchcraft. The events of nature were incomprehensible for the human being; when the sun disappeared in an eclipse, converted a day into a short night, the seasons followed one to each other in a synchronic way, unknown cosmic events, the human being realized that the nature palpitates full of life going through the moon phases. The occult forces acted in favor and against the humans, and, when those forces unleashed themselves, the human being had to find the way of calming them down in different rituals.

The human beings learned how to use fire and adore it; they also discovered the solar paces which define the seasons and periods of life, they cultivated and hunted, worshiped the benevolent deities which lavished sustenance on them, intuited the attraction of similar by obtaining abundance, identified the God of Hunting as a horned man with his horns shaped like a reindeer, or, they also identified Diana as the goddess of Nature, represented by the moon, as a symbol of fertility to increase the cultivation.

The phallic rituals appeared to express their gratitude to the goddess Earth ZARUNA (*mother of fertility*) for giving her wastefulness and abundance, just like they adored God the Father ZARUCH "*The Benefactor of Life*".

The rituals of gratitude were created, priests, priestesses, wise men, witches, wizards, shamans, the "*chosen ones*", initiated ones, ambassadors between humanity and deities, those which were in charge of adoring deities and teaching their designs. The knowledge of the paces of the life added to the gratitude for harvesting, allowed the origin of WICCA: the ancient religion of the harmony of life.

Today, thousands of supporters of the ancient magic give thanks to The God (*father*) and The Goddess (*mother*) for the wonder of existence.

WICCA'S MAGIC DATES

The Celts and the Druids, all of them knowledgeable like no one else of the celestial positions, set up the solar year according to the seasons, they understood those instants in which the cosmic cycles change, the exact moment to sow, the perfect time to harvest, the day for hunting; they discovered the power of the elements hidden into every human being.

By contemplating the cosmos, the position of the stars indicated the course of the seasons, God the Father Sun showed up his smile, and the Druids dedicated him the most important dates, they also discovered that the plants emulated the celestial position when the changes made by the moon and the earth had influence on the harvest, some of those plants expelled their scent only when there was a full moon, as well, they understood observing the changes in nature, that those changes worked equally in the human being.

They mixed the elements and prepared their first potions, found out the ability of talking to magical creatures and dancing with fairies, they made the fields to increase their limitless abundance, learned the magic of the unknown hidden in everything that we can see. Finally, the valuable is the invisible.

They lived in harmony with nature, dancing in the summer days, expressing gratitude to God the Father and Mother Goddess, until ignorance condemned them for living peacefully. They were condemned of heresy and subdued to die in the fire.

However, despite of the time, the Wiccan knowledge lives on; the voices were silenced but the thoughts were not. For many years, Wicca was hidden, silent, working in the shadows and available only for a few initiated.

Currently, the awakening of the Age of Aquarius revives the old traditions and The Wicca is slowly taking its place but rapidly out casting a series of beliefs and dogmas which don't contribute to the harmony of human beings with the cosmos.

The dawn of knowledge awakes for those that wish radical changes in their lives, advance and progress won't be long once humanity harmonize with nature and synchronize themselves with the cosmos, everyone will turn into a priest, a wizard or a witch of its own

personal realization getting to be the creator of its own universe, the abundance of Mother Goddess will be limitless benefactor.

WICCA'S KNOWLEDGE

The essence of the knowledge is present in the harmony of the strength of the inferior with the superior, using the law of similarities to work and increase a specific mental or physical alteration, the similar attract each other in many graduations, the abundance is present as in small and big things, it will depend on your state of mind.

Magic is unique, it does not have polarity, it has as a principle to materialize the thoughts changing your ideas into reality and obtain benefits. These arts depend on the intention of the practitioner, the same ritual that protects today, may destroy tomorrow.

At the beginning of the Age of Aquarius, the curiosity about the practices of mental power and occult knowledge impetuous emerged without fear or being condemned; today the walls of limitation have collapsed, and the ancient religion Wicca has woken up from its lethargy.

Millions of people daily irradiate their psychic energy by expending hours sitting in front of a computer; the art of creating using the mind will be more and more powerful. The window is opening up to an unknown and amazing world, taking us to know the modern witchcraft through the internet, only those who possess the required knowledge will get to progress and be a part of the change.

The needs of the spirit grow; it is the Wicca's renaissance, the harmony with nature. Without a doubt, the magic of the thoughts will be the science to prevail in the future. It is necessary to be ready, the knowledge of the spirit is the way to get success in reunite our humanity.

Men was born as a creator, thought in which, the *"whole"* learns to become perfect every time. Returning to Wicca, is to go deeper inside of our heart, it is to be reborn looking at the universe, and feeling ourselves as cosmopolitans, habitants of the cosmos.

DIANA AND THE FERTILITY

The woman, the living icon of the creation, she was subdued and limited, condemned since antiquity, without acknowledgement that is her who generates growth and fertility. The woman was the price to pay for Wicca when she died in the fire, condemned just for being a woman.

The moon phases regulate the cycles of ovulation, making the energy that flows from her body to increase or decrease, for example: At the moment of cooking, the food gets impregnated with her feelings, it also depends on the menstrual cycle.

Parapsychology searches the great ability of women to generate paranormal phenomenon, such as premonition, telepathy, psychic healing, and therefore her role is prevailing for every magical work.

The woman was in charge of the preparation of potions and unguents in the rituals of Wicca's magic, she was the force of the femininity and fertility, she was who attracted abundance to the harvest, just like she was the one who weaved the talisman of power for her man, the sailor, the hunter, as protection and fortune.

Afterwards, those who knew the power enclosed in a woman, did its best to keep her away from the rest, also, if she was in her menstrual cycle was judged such as dirty or ceremonially unclean.

(Leviticus 12, 1-5)

Jehovah said to Moses:
Say to the Israelites:
A woman who becomes pregnant and gives birth to a son will be ceremonially unclean for seven days, just as she is unclean during her monthly period. On the eighth day the boy is to be circumcised. Then the woman must wait thirty-three days to be purified from her bleeding. She must not touch anything sacred or go to the sanctuary until the days of her purification are over.

If she gives birth to a daughter, for two weeks the woman will be unclean, as during her period. Then she must wait sixty-six days to be purified from her bleeding.

What kind of difference exists between giving birth to a boy or a girl? Given that life has no differences, maybe since then, the persecution against women emerged. (*Read the book "**A trip to The Apocalypse**"*)

However, this sentence has been alive for a very long time, stunning and marginalizing woman in the magic works as in the social life. In the latest years, woman has earned the place that she deserves, she advances toward the road with a great effort, and perhaps, it is time to appreciate the magical power that exists in every woman.

Witchcraft is the essence of the feminine gender, of the creator. It is expected that the pages of this book open the doors of life, in order to make the woman valuable not because of her body but because of her essence of magical life.

The woman/man equilibrium turns out to be the greatest strength, just for being the living representation of Mother Goddess and God the Father.

SECRETS OF MAGIC

In order to discover the secrets that allow the use of the regent elements of nature, it is necessary to unify the strength of the spirit with the magic of the thought, getting to know the Master and the power of the mind.

The Master: witchcraft without an awakening to spirituality is the equivalent to putting a powerful weapon of the world on a fool's hands.

There is a parallel world which in, there is an odd temple, the cradle of the spiritual knowledge, called Shamballah, for millenniums it's being a part of the spirit's culture and philosophy, nobody knows where it is, a monk lives within, his name is *Kadaisha*, the Master.

Religions without God, like Wicca, Taoism and Buddhism, talk about the Master who rests in every being and awakes to show us a way in the inexorable passage of time. I have invited *Kadaisha* to guide with his knowledgeable thoughts the pages of this book. He invites us, not to follow him but to enter into our own temple, that one hidden deep inside the heart.

The Master **Kadaisha** *said:*

"In the deepest darkness, the humblest light is a sun; you must always walk toward the light".

Every sentence from the Master encourages us to think over; to stop for a while our desire and eagerness, his thoughts will be the sign to show us the right path towards ourselves, to disclose the power of the mind.

Let's use the sleeping knowledge of our inner self so we can reach the scepter of the magic and the power to manage the elements and their elementals. In this way, our lives will be fulfilled of wealth greater than the worldly staff.

The art of magic is not learned in a moment, on the contrary, practicing will allow us for understanding the way it works, as soon as we get it, we'll reach the highest goals. *"We will not want to possess anything else"*. On this point, a bit of philosophy is important, life is not about the material possessions, we get caught up, our luggage must be as light as the wind, or, on the other hand, our existence could not be based on living but in taking care of the possessions we have amassed, and, whether we like it or not, we'll have to let them go when we die.

Magic has a hidden demon, it is **"The Power"**; when the assurance of the preparation for the different rituals increases and we see their magical results, the power will possess us, and consequently, avarice and greed will come.

While the equilibrium gets lost in material possessions, we will lose everything including ourselves. Let's use magic to enforce the spirit but not the body, the material possessions are ephemeral, the ones of the spirit are eternal.

*The Master **Kadaisha** said:*

"Imagination is the most powerful weapon in magic, that is why you must be careful what you wish for".

Let's get inside the magical world of Wicca's knowledge, as a suggestion: go slowly, take this subject easy, do not hurry, only this way you will make magic flow in its total power, and remember that everything has its own time in nature.

CHAPTER II

THE WIZARD'S CRUCIBLE

«Only those who look with the heart's eyes will find out what is really valuable»

The unification of the mind and the elements are generated when the Wizard harmonizes himself with nature by a ceremony or a ritual, calling upon the regent energies of the cosmos. This way, the wizard obtains the strength from the superior and the inferior, working with the power of imagination over the mind and the substance. The continuous practices of this experience are the different rituals of Magick.

In Wicca, the different rituals are made according to some dates, the moon phases and the seasons. Every ritual has the same principle, although it differs of the practice of the rules and elements used for their realization.

Since the ancient times of the hyperborean culture and posterior traditions, the expression *"Magick"* is the representation of a magical law, *"Do whatever you consider to do"*; it's accepted the unlimited use of the natural powers in order to carry out the free desire

of "*doing*". The acceptance of this law represents the knowledge of the laws of magic.

The ritual is individual or collective, in the last case, we´ll have a guide to direct the group; in the individual ritual, the officiant and the guide is the same person, having more power than in the collective ritual due to the mental neatness for the executions of the acts, on the other side, in the collective ritual some of the participating easily lose their concentration, giving themselves negative energies or mental encumbrances which make the magical practice difficult.

Maturity is necessary to carry out collective rituals, they have a great erotic component, and it should be managed according to the desire. The feeling of love releases itself in sensitive people. Getting by without the judgment of the conscience, the strength of the elements generates and attraction that awakes sensuality.

It is suggested that before taking place in a collective ritual to take in account what you wish to obtain and your moral state of mind, there isn´t an intention to judge, condemn or limit each one´s desires.

Disagreeing with many beliefs, a relationship which is supported by the true love in harmony with nature enriches spiritually, it would be convenient that the ritual to be carried out be by couples sharing the same purpose.

Procreation is the most intense ritual; it is the realization of love and not a single fleeting and instinctive game. The art of loving becomes the most deep and complex ceremony of magic. In witchcraft, sexuality as well as the respect for the couple is above every concept, being this fact, the first act of power shown by nature: giving life.

At different magic dates like Beltane, the intimate relations are more frequent, it depends on each participant without lessening the femininity or increasing the manhood. The real wizard keeps itself in harmony with nature, maintaining the equilibrium between female and male. (*Read: **Tantra Magic and Sexuality***).

It is important to keep in mind whether a couple wants to conclude a ritual with an intimate relation, they should foresee the risk of pregnancy; Wicca in its knowledge does not procreate by mistake but as an answer to the law of the life. Each couple will know when the right moment comes, only the true love and responsibility mark the new procreations.

In early times, sexuality was enjoyed using a variety of plants as contraceptive methods, at present that is easier and pleasure is greater, it deeply depends on the desire; the intimate relations subsequent to a ritual should be just that: a ritual of true love, of dedication without hurry, without limitations to the gift of giving to each other, making the woman to achieve and unleash her whole power.

KINDS OF MAGIC

Goetia or Dark magic, it attracts the spirits of dead people, negative energies which are destructive, even for the mind who calls on them; it works with the same rituals and elements of the White Magic but focused on destruction, as well as making animal sacrifices in order to obtain power, it does not have limits nor is it loyal, treachery and greed are stigmas of those who practice it; love does not exist for the Black Magic but rather as the violation of sexuality causing mental damages to those who participate in it.

Be careful of succumbing in those groups… The damage caused by them is irremediable, ending in suicide, if you want to learn about magic, be your own performer, remember that magic has no masters nor there exists anyone as powerful as yourself.

Theurgia or Light magic, the art of manipulating energies of the elements with the purpose of improving the life, either the need to resort to destruction, they are known as «*The Angelic Forces*», the four powers: Fire, Earth, Air and Water, ruled by the four princes, Seraph, Ariel, Cherub and Tharsis. The power of love increases, and the creating force returns multiplied to its practitioner, abundance makes itself present without mediation of pain and those who practice light magic find out the power in the simplicity of life; there is something important to consider, dark magic have no action over the white one, on the contrary, the magic of love overrides negative energies of dark magic, although it requires confidence.

Theurgia and Goetia are two names, ultimately they are the same magic, and they only change by the intention of the operator. Nobody, not even Solomon himself, would find the frontier between dark magic and light magic. However, similar divinations are carried out with both of them. If a person with a mental disturbance and a life full of grudges tries to carry out a work of light magic, even if using Theurgia, this work would be black due to the energy emanated in the person's mind.

The oriental philosophy of Tao shows us the harmonic union of The Whole, light and darkness, the creating principle of nature between the receptive (*white*) and the creative (*black*); in other words, male and female, without mentioning sex, but the active principle of the generating polarity, positive and negative.

It is recognized as Light magic, all those rituals which imply the construction of abundance, wellness, fortune, love. Dark magic uses the same formula, but, it destroys, separates, causes losses and illnesses, kills, produces hate and rancor, deprivation and misery.

Good and evil are just an individual concept, the opposite sides of freedom. It depends on each one to consider what is good or evil.

Magic ignores these concepts, it's one in its essence, it depends on the heart's feelings. While projecting

psychic energies and realizing wishes, those energies will return stronger to their creator, irradiating it along with his thoughts; analyze the kind of magic you are working with, if you look for good, good will return; if you look for evil, evil will return for you and for those who are in your mental sphere.

*The Master **Kadaisha** said:*

"Before the unexpected and the unknown, fear is the nest of evil; if you feel fear of the road, appease your spirit and then walk it".

Rituals release the force of the Elements and the power of the spirits, they attract the angels that govern the forces, producing the transmuting potion. Inside the wizard´s mind, the crucible of power releases its force.

ZARUNA'S INFLUENCE

Due to its power, the moon has been known as Selene, Goddess of fertility, abundance and growth, to receive its influence.

The Phases of the Moon: While the moon rotates around the earth, it shows the same face, and sometimes, according to its position, the moon is seen with certain grades of illumination, taking into account the corresponding moon phase, these phases as a whole are known as the synodic month.

The new moon: The moon, while being between the sun and the earth becomes almost invisible. "*The age of the moon*" begins at this point.

The waxing moon: When the moon gets her first 7, 4 days, reaches the phase called half-moon. It looks slightly illuminated only in one of its borders; the rest of it shows the shadow produced by the earth's curvature.

The full moon: At the end of 14 days, the moon looks thoroughly illuminated resembling a disc. Depending on the season, this phase can be seen closer or further from earth.

The waning moon: accomplished 22,1 days since the new moon, the moon can be seen the opposite way than the waxing moon, a dark border and the rest of it illuminated; the cycle will be completed after 29,53 days, this cycle is called the synodic month.

The human body is similar to the planet earth; it's composed of 74% water, and in turn is altered by the gravitational moon's influence. The cerebral micro-marshes are caused by the moon phase, as a result showing some mood swings. It also influences women near to giving birth to delay or speed up the labor.

At full moon nights, there is some psychological behavior changes, acting as «*animals*»; werewolves and vampires are samples of that attitude known as lycanthropy. Such alteration was considered as a diabolical or spiritual possession, a very useful argument increasing the belief of those who assume the fight between the divine and diabolical forces.

Wizards and witches know the close bond between the earth and the moon, taking advantage of their cosmic positions to carry out rituals of Magick, as well as the farmers who know the appropriate moment for sowing, harvesting and the right compost to use according to the moon phase. Births are also ruled by the phases of the moon.

Unlike some specific rituals like magnetized candles or mirrors, just like certain characteristics of the moon, Magick or Wicca take into consideration the moon phases known as solstice or equinox, the forces of the four elements: Fire, Earth, Air and Water are always implicit in every ritual; making the rituals much more powerful during the key dates at the apex of each season or Sabbat.

Keep in mind that the phase of the moon or apex goes only for two hours, the point of interface or interval is produced three days and a half after the last phase.

Example:

The full moon is in its total phase the first day of a month: at that moment the drop begins to the interval phase, this means that the way to the waning moon has begun, even if the moon looks totally full, after three and a half days the moon has changed, locating itself at the interval point between a phase and another. After this day, or interval, the progress to the new phase begins, this phase is totally produced after three and a half days. This also means that the rituals to be made during the different equinoxes or solstices must start to be prepared three days before the phase as such. That is the way to be totally harmonized with nature.

• **The new moon. (Equinox):** It is the ideal time to initiate rituals for: beginning, new business and love. Stillness is present at this phase, the mind is receptive, wishes gain strength, and it is a good time to light yellow candles and/or wearing clothes of the same color. Its influence is more powerful during the summer.

• **The waxing moon. (Equinox):** The growing and beginnings are gestated during this phase. It is the ideal time to make prosperity rituals, salary increases, new home, brewing in the thoughts the seed of desire.

• **The full moon. (Solstice):** Empowers the action, most of the rituals are done during this phase. It alters the senses and increases liquids, the person is relatively easier to be affected. The rituals to be made at this time are about love, telepathic influence and spells.

• **The waning moon. (Solstice):** The moon force has fallen, it's time to sow and prune, liquids have descended, everything is under decreasing, and the mind and body have a receptive attitude. It is the ideal time to practice rituals for new wishes. The love will be asleep, the seeds of illusion are reaped while waning, and whenever the moon evolves toward the new moon, rituals get strength until it reaches the apex of the full moon becoming them reality.

ZARUCH'S INFLUENCE

The God of Light, essence of life, the power of the magnanimous. The sun generates an influence depending on the earth rotation's where each element works in each and every season releasing certain forces. The ellipsis formed by the earth on its trip around the sun has the winter solstice in its aphelion, the moment in which it is further from the sun, corresponding to the 23rd of December; and its perihelion, the moment of being closest to the sun, corresponding to the summer solstice on the 23rd of June. The equinoxes take part among the solstices, the summer one on the 23rd of March, and the fall one on the 23rd of September. As of these points, the four seasons are born being ruled by each element. While a season begins to decrease, the next season increases at the same time. The four earth positions in front of the sun are used in Magick to practice the four great Sabbats. The four seasons entail the secrets of life and death.

Summer:

The renewal, the selection of the strongest, abundance of time, and the igneous element unleash the elementals of fire, the salamanders guided by **Djin.** It relates to transformation, it is a propitious time for moving and running new business, it's time for new affective relationships. Summer attracts fleeting illusions, it's a time to be cautious because this period precedes the mutation and great changes. The Fire element is enforced by the summer, and at the same time the fire is rekindled by the fall Air element. The 23rd of June is the most important date on the summer solstice.

Fall:

This season comes with the subtle strength of the first breezes, even though they are refreshing, are also the announcement of the Air element; hurricanes come on this season transforming nature, avoiding the old things,

carrying the seeds of the new, cleaning up the ashes from the summer. The aerial element releases its elementals: Sylphs, Sylphids and Zephyrs; governed by Paralda. It's time for savings and love, most of the animals perceive its presence, so they begin to accumulate food to be prepared for the cool winter. Species start their mating process for the new life which will come in the spring. The fall equinox happens about the 23rd of September, when the cosmos forces and the Air element join together by an amazing reawakening power.

Winter:

Nobody knows its initial moment; it just comes hidden into a cold zephyr, an almost imperceptible breeze. Symbol of the aquatic element, releases the water elementals: Undines, Nodites and Nereides; governed by **Neckna**. A layer made of ice crystals covers nature. The ground and the trees have lost their splendor.

The hibernation process begins, everything is asleep, nature feels its presence and the human mind feels it too; these are strange days, animals hide themselves in caverns to put up with the cold. The distance of the earth in regards to the sun makes the energy to flow in a different way, it's the ideal moment for mental creations. The winter solstice takes place on the 23rd of December.

Spring:

The earth sets out on its journey back to the sun, the sleeping life is awakening; plants, animals and thoughts are reborn, the land is beneficial, the womb starts with its labor. The terrestrial element releases the earth elementals: magical beings and gnomes; governed by Leprechaun. It's time of prosperity, of birth, it's the continuity of life. The spring equinox takes place on the 23rd of March.

SABBATS

Samhain

The end of the agricultural year is celebrated on the **31st of October** according to The Witches' Wiccan Wheel, it's the moment wherein nature starts the process of regenerating the new life, symbolizes death and life, the continuous wheel of gestation, the solemn festival known as Samhain is produced, it comes as a representation of the death of the harvest and the repose of the land to take shape for the new life on winter.

The days before Samhain, women used to ride a sort of peg while they plowed the field; actually, such practice still prevails. From this ritual originate the legends according to which witches rode their brooms, likewise the role of men is to carry out the hunt's dancing in a reindeer costume, emerging the Goatman myths, symbol of Demon.

Towards midnight is made the Akelarre, it's a Basque origin word whose translation is "the goat meadow". The participants were disguised, hunters covered up their bodies with reindeer skin, and women made up themselves for the celebration as an act of gratitude for the received harvest from Diana and Faun. They celebrated the end of the Celtic year which culminated adoring Bacchus, the God of Wine.

(As additional information and according to Wicca: Witchcraft is the attraction of the similar, for this reason men were in reindeer costumes in order to get closer and hunt them, just like the phallic rituals which are related to fertilization).

The goat meadow or field was the favorite place to perform their festivity, being very careful of looking for the witches' circles which before were known as the Devil's footprints, but today people know that it's just a fungus that spreads out; being more notorious at the beginning of winter.

Samhain symbolized the death and beginning of the new life, that day was used to commemorate God the Father and Mother Goddess for the continuity of the existence.

"A/N

We have altered life's natural pace through human vanity; Wicca through its wisdom passed on to us a deep knowledge of harmony between humans and nature, perhaps, and because of it, we have lost the compass and have disoriented ourselves. We changed dates and have desynchronized the time, that's why the advance and progress of humanity have been tarnished by such many disasters.

Why is the 31st of October the end of the year instead of 31st of December? July and August are a couple of months imposed by the romans, they replaced the tenth month (December) by October which really and naturally is the eighth month, and finally December took place as the twelfth month. They moved away the beginning of winter, considered by the Celts "the instant in which the earth falls asleep to gestate the new life". The solar year begins in winter.

In the middle of the VIII century, the Catholic Church attempted to Christianize the Samhain celebration, referring to the 31st of October as the Demon's adoration night, and declaring the 1st of November the All Saint's day and All Hallows' Day. The 31st of October is celebrated by the Catholic Church the popular festivity

All Hallows' Eve or All Saints' Eve, as time went by it became Halloween.

To delve into the topic of the Inquisition and desecration of the freedom of thought, during the same 13th century during the "March of peasants", the Pope Innocent the IV established the death at the stake. Condemning witchcraft as a heresy to the church (honor to those who died because of the ignorance of the Church).

Witchcraft begins in the Genesis of humanity, the Anglo-Saxons called it Wicca or the Old Religion, that word designated the work of the wise, the experts of the secrets of nature. Over time the English word "witch" derives from the same linguistic root than "wit" and "wise" started to be used.

Sorcery lost its direction when merged with cults, pseudo-religions and dogmas, deforming its magical content, introducing unnecessary elements to the practice of rituals, and even worse, mixing drugs, music, sex, sacrifices, etc. The real sorcery does not require victims in their rituals.

Yule

Winter Solstice, 23rd of December

The magic of the cosmos' power is performed during the winter solstice towards the 23rd of December starting on the 20th day when everything is prepared for the first day of the new harvest's birth. During this day occurs the longest night and the shortest day of the year. It is then celebrated as the return of the light, the birth of the seed. It's important to clarify that religions use this day to supposedly celebrate the birth of Jesus; moreover it should be noted that there is no data in existence to support its veracity.

During the winter solstice or Yule, the Wicca directly connect to the spirit, to the inner self; it's the moment to be influenced by the Water element, so the earth in the silence of the winter night gestates life into her.

The rituals practiced during this time are focused on the inner awakening, wisdom flows from the inside, it's time for meditation, uniting families and celebrating the dinner of the lights during the longest night of the year. The purpose of performing rituals during these days have the intention of inner harmony in order to prepare for the life's return and the new spring.

Lights and bonfires are ignited while dancing around in circles counterclockwise, or to the left singing or reciting different prayers to Mother Goddess and God the Father.

On this celebration date, the house is decorated with mistletoe and green plants or pines which will last the entire winter; perhaps from this festivity the legends of Santa Claus and the Christmas tree were born.

Giving presents to each other is synonymous of abundance; rituals of interior harmonization are practiced during the night of the 24th on the new sunrise, it's necessary to be at peace with others, hoping that the new light comes full of prosperity. It is important not to confuse this Sabbat with the religious belief of Christmas.

Imbolc

Since the 2nd until the 4th of February
Darkness gives way to light, days are equal to nights, harmony has awakened and it announces the presence of the spring wherein the life gestated on winter is born. The first water drops melt in minuscule riverbeds shining like diamonds, Imbolc has arrived.

Sunrise is earlier and everything turns green, small seeds begin to slowly germinate and the first sprouts fill everything around. It is the ideal time to prepare for the new life.

Likewise in this day, the works for the entire Wiccan year are prepared, the tools are cleaned and the process to release what is attached begins, the home-elements must be changed of place and the last day of January is the preparation of the fortune breads.

For Wicca, it is a time of dedication and strength, everything awakens to welcome the Goddess Mother Nature announcing the spring's arrival. Everybody shares the bread rolls and crumbs are throwing into the wind as a symbol of the forthcoming prosperity. Green and yellow clothes decorate the first warm sunbeams which come to warm up the cold wind saying good bye to the winter. The time and the cycles pass, and already the light covers everything, nature's intimacy in creation is near to be discovered, and at that point the nakedness of life will show up.

Thereby, during these days it is also recommended to fix and decorate the house in expectation of the arrival of abundance.

Ostara

23rd of March, Spring Equinox
Since the 21st until the 24th
The working season has come, the wise Goddess Mother takes refuge late and awakes early, and now days are longer, birds are the first to bring us a happy sunrise, during these days the ritual of the purifying egg is practiced by passing the egg along the body before the first rays of the sun illuminate.

The cold is gone and the trees are covered with small outbreaks of sprouts of new flowers, the Wicca discovers the sleeping awake of life, and simultaneously enters the Fire element announcing in the Aries constellation the strength of the life giving birth to the summer.

During these days the activities must be defined by happiness and enthusiasm; according to the Celts and Druids this is a special day to release dark energies trapped in our spirit, in case of being in harmony with the cosmos we should on the 23rd of March in the spring give fresh eggs.

It is season to pick up the first bouquets of flowers; they will be a symbol of love and attraction. Women

who collect the first 7 flowers from spring and put them underneath the pillow will dream about their future love and happiness and fortune will come to their lives. If you want to know more rituals to easily practice on spring or another season according to your needs, read: Grandma's Magical Book.

Beltane

30th of April

The infinite mind of God the Father and Mother Goddess are unified with the body; the skin awakes the desire of fertility, love and sensuality give way to attraction, the field are fertilized with the power of feelings, it is a season in which to discover sex without fear and without limitations, the total surrender and emulation of nature to the cooling of the Earth with new desires.

Sex is implemented to the new life preceding summer, the Hindu culture and Tantrism the Sacred Sexuality make emphasis on this date in which Kundalini Spirit awakes unwinding for strength and energy to manipulate Mother Goddess Nature's powers. (*Read the book: Magic and Sexuality – The Power of Sex*).

This is a prosperous date for the initiation of magical arts.

The ancient Wicca suggested that during the following three days to pin some small stakes near trees, as a phallic representation of fertilization, according to the old rituals you should pin a stake near a tree per year of life, men and women may carry out this ritual, it is recommended to dig as much holes as the number of years you have lived.

Phallic symbols correspond to female and male sexual organs, it is good to make hot chocolate the night of the 30th of April, and then read what appears at the bottom of the cup.

Remember that the chocolate's power is also related to the phallic representation of the pot and *whisk (*olleta y molinillo*).

The night of love and sexuality for those who wish to do so, should try this old ritual from Wicca and Tantrism:

• Take 7 flowers, three red, three yellow, and one white.
• Scented oil
• Sandalwood

- Cinnamon
- Three river stones
- Salt and water

The two days before, you must set the scented oil with the cinnamon and the sandalwood to receive the morning sun, with the purpose to be charged with the forces of life.

The 30th of April at around 9 p.m. the couple will find and intimate place and dedicate to discover each other's spirit through their skin the following way:

The white flower is set on the woman's abdomen (*being naked*), and the three stones have to be placed forming a triangle with one on the abdomen and the other two toward the breasts. The rest of the flowers are placed forming a circle around the couple, next the man takes the oil to anoint the woman's body without possessing her, and he only goes along her body using his hands while pronouncing:

> Mother Goddess reflected
> on the body of life
> My hands plow the fields
> of the sleeping fertility

To awake love
Here I sow love seeds
In the union of my soul
In the sigh of the sea
In a kiss from the dawn
I love you and love the fruit
that lurks in your belly.

The man gets closer to the woman like looking for his beloved's body, moving his own body like a snake, crawling, he gets his chest closer and closer to hers, moves rhythmically, he starts moving his oiled body on top of hers, avoiding to possess her.

Afterwards, he takes the white flower and removes its petals off and spills them over the woman's chest like spilling the seed.

Subsequently, sitting in front of each other, the woman takes the stones, the water and the salt, and says:

For the God the Father who fertilizes the land
For He who is the salt of life Carried in the seed
I receive the thoughts of love and the seed of life
By salt and water that will be for eternity
Fertilizing my spirit with your spirit and my soul

Will be a part of your soul and your spirit will be a part of my spirit

Holding hands, they both let their beings to flow like the river; they will give themselves to each other feelings the love of life.

Subsequently, the three stones must be taken near a tree, which it was previously surrounded by the flower petals. Right there and then, you give each other a stone, the third one, must be buried at the roots of the tree.

The stones must be kept as a souvenir of their pact of love.

Wicca says: If after practicing this ritual, the couple really love each other and they stay together solving difficulties, prosperity and great happiness will come to them, additionally it is possible that infidelity does not have place in their relationship.

Litha

Summer Solstice, 23rd of June
Beginning on the 21st and ending on the 24th
God the Father finds shelter in heaven; the sun shines in its entire splendor irradiating strength on the season in which nature irradiates its entire splendor. The earth is at its closest point to the sun receiving the emanations of life.

This is the time in which everything flows in total harmony; summer releases the sleeping secrets of inner beauty that opens to love and limitless dedication.

On this date Wicca celebrates one of the most spectacular rituals of magic, in the evening hours on the 23rd of June they light circular bonfires representing the force of Fire.

The Litha Sabbat takes the power of fire to be accumulated in the different elements; originally it is accumulated in candles. This is the initial day to magnetize the candles to be used in different rituals, considering that you may need only one for using it to light the rest of them during the different sabbats.

The solar force irradiates all its entire power, parallel to this, changes occur along with the transformations of nature. During summer, nature frees all creation during the previous winter, giving life to life, the abundance is present to be used by wizards those who keep trapped in the cosmos' force all the time, released at the time when the wizard needs the total power of fire.

During the summer evenings magic gathers around the fire, giving way to the emanations and the presence of salamanders to purify everything that has been accumulated, due to this virtue the Litha Sabbat is extremely important.

One of the most profound rituals of the Wiccan magic consists in the following:

On the night of the solstice, take a piece of clothing impregnated with the person's energy, preferably a used sheet which has not been washed; extending it out on the night of the 23rd, and setting on it petals of yellow flowers in a circular shape, in the middle of the circle a red candle, and 33 pins are also needed.

The person should sit in the center of the circle of flowers, focusing on the interior life and its different limitations, circumstances. Once sited, proceed to encircle the body with the pins, afterwards moisturize your body with water. It is a symbolic way to release parasite energies.

In a meditative attitude, the mental burden is released, it is best to do this ritual naked, later, fold the hands and focused on the interior (*go with in*), invoke the Fire Energies:

> On this Sabbat I celebrate Litha's
> day with magical rituals,
> I invoke you Great Mother Goddess,
> Great God the Father,
> This is the purifying time.
> The past destinies have laggedbehind,
> It is the purifying time.

The whole essence vibrates with its energy
Fire comes back giving warmth and life.

Father Sun
Light up my darkness, Bring light to my life
Fill me up with your essence of light
So the darkness with all its secrets
be revealed to me.

Transmute
Oh Heavenly King, Useless into useful
Dark into light, Ignorance into wisdom
Ward off from me pain, Hesitation and sadness

Let me be like you, Transmuter of life.

Purify me!
Purify me!
Purify me!

Taking the red candle and looking into the flame, say:

For the Force of Creation, For the Mother Goddess
For God the Father, For the purifying Fire
For the sun, For the moon, For the lights of the sky
For the magic and the enchantment

Of the Fire, Of the Earth
Of the Air, Of the water

Everything which is trapped in darkness now
(say the next words witha great mental force)
Is transmuted into light purified to Fire
Engendered by Water, Resurrected on Earth
Released in Air
Every dark situation from
my past is now clear in my mind.

Thanks Father
Thanks Mother
For blessing this creature made by you
Thanks to you
For the wisdom of light
For the hope of tomorrow
For the illusion of being alive
To culminate my work.

Completing the above, proceed as follows:

Get up with caution of the pins, fold the sheet taking the four points to the center, while using the candle for light, make sure that the petals stay inside the sheet, after that you must fold four more times in the same way to finally

seal by letting drops of wax fall on the center where the points meet. Afterward throw the sheet to a water current taking care of not getting hurt with the pins.

Rituals of transmutation and purification are made on the Summer Solstice and during Litha.

Lughnassad

1st of August
The Earth awakes up throwing seeds and fruits out; it is the first harvest's season, the Mother Goddess' kindness and fertility, bring us nourishment not just for the body, but for the mystical renovation, showing us that the gift of the real abundance is giving, without limits, without accumulating, retaining or possession. On the contrary, kindness opens wide, it's the magical harvest, it's the fruit, it's the wheat delivered a thousand for one.

It's the time of the life's resurrection, the Mother Goddess discloses her nakedness and delivers the fruit of the womb, it's the origin, the continuity of the miracle of life.

On the first of August the earth changes leaving summer getting into fall, It's the day of Lughnassad, it's the gratitude from humanity to the earth's fertility, Diana the Mother Goddess delivers the hidden seed in the fruit to all beings, the infinite nourishment of wisdom is delivered too.

This is the magical Sabbat of abundance, it's time for preparation of new bread, nourishment for the body as well as for the soul. After Litha when the sun wakes up and delivers light, where the purifying fire has prepared the life's crucible, the moment to knead the sacred flour, rituals that are held this day are fused on increasing and abundance.

As gratitude to the Gods for the received harvest and to ask for wisdom for the upcoming sowing, as well it is the moment to invoke the four guardians of the watchtowers of the elements to make them benign in the continuity of life, do the following ritual:

Let's do an altar, it could be done on the dinner table and decorated with a white tablecloth, placing on all four corners fruits surrounded by flowers.

As a center piece we'll set some wheat spikes in the form of a triangle and inside of it make some circles of corn, it's important to get 12 pieces of bread to place 3 of them on each corner as a representation of the wholeness of nourishment for feeding mind, body and spirit. With humility, we will give the two main chairs to the Goddess Mother and God the Father; as creatures born of the earth we will honor the body which should be lightly covered or preferably naked.

On each side of the triangle made of spikes we'll light two candles (*a white one and a black one*), that way the balance will be perfect between the forces of nature.

Subsequently, we'll do the following on the center piece:

Taking a spike from each side of the triangle, raise the hands and say:

Here is the first grain from the first harvest
We thank you God Father-Mother
For the bread, fruit from this spike
For the nourishment to the body
For the nourishment to the soul
For the abundance received.
Oh mother, lady of the fields
Fertility and constant life
Without limits deliver your essence
To feed your creatures.
Hoping it is not only my body
To which you care
Give me enough wisdom
To plant new seed and so continue with life
Show me the path of eternal autumn.

That is already close
To deliver in your hands the new seed
And in the cold winds preceding winter
Send you my gratitude,
Mother-Father of mine.

Keep your hands raised and at this instant let your mind quiet dawn, remember the - benefits earned, shake the spikes and let the wheat grains - fall down on the altar, keep in mind - the first grains so later you collect them and keep them in a green little bag to be hung behind the door.

Place the spikes down and take the candles, the black one with the right hand and the white one with the left hand saying the following invocation:

Oh, Goddess of the stars twinkling at night
Oh, Lord of the rain and the winds
Oh, shining star that lights up the sky
Oh, Goddess of the sleeping dark moon
Show me the power of the soul's resurrection
Show me the power of the substance's resurrection
Just like the tree dies in the seed.

Just like the seed is born as a tree
Show me to transmute death into life.

Make these flames which are symbol of light and
hope, constantly shine in my spirit to understand
The secrets of life and darkness, sow and harvest
Past and future.
The eternal secrets of the way to wisdom
Give me the gift of living in balance
Between night and day.

Taking the corn grains and pointing at the chairs dedicated to Goddess and God say:

This grain
Fruit from the first harvest
Is united with my life essence
As eternal wisdom nourishment
Thank you Father-Mother
For this granted gift
Recalling the continuity of life

Recalling the absence of death
I take this grain to be seeded
And planted in the earth's womb
As life's resurrection
In the earth's entrails

In silence and respectfully look at the grains and think what would happen if they all disappear from this world. Consider that the equilibrium of life is about giving and receiving, that the continuity of nature is eternal wisdom, there is no death, - just hope for the new spring to wave the sky. Tie the bread, spikes, corn and candles up with the same spikes like making a sort of nest; the next morning - bury everything preferably near- a waterbed, if it is not possible bury it in the meadow. Save

the remaining grains until next year, at moments of prayer offer them to God and Goddess by placing them on the chairs and later bury them.

Mabon

Fall Equinox, 23rd of September
Since the 21st until the 24th
Fall has arrived, the point that breaks the balance, and starts preparing for winter, earth is collected, the trees drop out the last leaves and everything seems prepared, like getting ready to go to sleep during the cold winter.

From this moment the sky changes, the sun - is now different with a touch of nostalgia and desolation, the harvest has come to an end, the Goddess Mother- now in the bellies of life that come in the spring.

The sun gives way to the beautiful Goddess Moon whose presence will remain longer for our enjoyment, from this day on, the nights will be longer and days - shorter and taciturn.

The whispering wind awakes Mabon not as death but as the discreet creation and silent life.

The existence flows now; God the Father and the Goddess Mother invite us on this date to walk towards the inner self just like nature does, it is time for meditation, for harmony and for peace; starts the season of concentration and - advent of the continuity of life.

The equilibrium of **LUGHNASSAD** has changed, the night passes its mantle and the Goddess Mother begins her retirement to refuge inside of herself brewing life, it is -mating time, love and attraction are everywhere, -bodies anxious of life get together by rituals of continuity, life makes its way, the resurrection starts slowly hidden in the bodies who love and fertility -smiles quietly, and the God Sun discrete and ashamed and perhaps a little jealous leaves. From this date forward the days are shorter and the moon Celestine of lovers becomes the nanny of - life lavishing care by making the nights longer, life sleep under the lulls of the night and - species hibernate, so, it is time that we enter within us.

It's time to discover the inner strength to create new ideas and to have projects.

The time of Mabon is without a doubt the line between light and darkness, the mysterious line of life and the apparent death, the silence and the cold winter are now present, the rituals of love are much more powerful if are practiced during this date. Likewise is time for covens to introduce the new members of the group or initiated, each coven has its own initiation rituals.

As the initiation periods begins for the young wizards and witches, this is the time or phase to collect some leaves and seed that has fallen from the trees, as well as water from a river. These elements will be used in the future for different magical preparations. For example: If you need to do a ritual for abundance, or an energetic cleaning.

When the seeds and plants collected in the autumn releases the regenerative force of life.

As a suggestion: get small fabric bags preferably black, to save the plants and seeds which must be thoroughly dry, as well as glass bottles to preserve the collected water which contains magical powers.

The same way as the Nile River changes its color on this date, the waters around the world are filled with energy.

In preparation for a new life, let's do a ritual for fall.

We need:

• Leaves
• Berries
• Seeds
• Flower petals
• Mineral oil or unscented
• Essential oil, i.e.
• Cinnamon
• Sandalwood
• Cedron
• Dry aromatic plants (*sweet*) herbs
• several small glass bottles for preparing the potions. Place all the plants in a basket and take them outside. Leave the basket out for 7 nights under the dew, to receive the last influence of the autumn equinox.

Days and nights are the same, but from the 23rd of September on the nights become longer; two days before Mabon put the plants into the glass bottles add soft fragrance and fill the battle with oil. They must be placed the bottles under the sun to receive the forces of the superior, then, save them to be used when needed.

Let's do an altar, if possible in an open field, in the afternoon, before it gets dark. The purpose is that the sunset arrives while the ritual is being performed

We just need some things from nature very easy to find, begin by drawing a circle with dry leaves and seeds; find some small stones to draw a second circle inside the first one, and some little wooden sticks to be used as stakes, place them around the circle.

Sit down in the middle of the circle, look at the sunset, focused on it and meditate about the upcoming changes, think that life is the constant renewal of continuity.

Sit in lotus position; place your hands on your knees. Remain in this position for the entire sunset, until almost dark. Keep in mind the first star you see, if the sky is cloudy and you can't see the stars try to focus on the light, when the scenery is between light and darkness say the following prayer:

Oh, God Sun now you sailing in the boat of days,
To the cold winter and the lonely melancholy.
The trees show their nakedness
And the cold winds come to life.
The dark night covers with her mantle
The fruit of the lovers
While the bellies are filled with life,
Your Goddess Mother shelters you
Getting dressed in white clothes
On the long nights of the cold night.
Everything gets quiet and calm
Everything is now an empty stillness
But I know It´s not like that
The cold winter is no more
of the new spring´s birth
Oh God Sun, take me on the life boat
To be like you and let the moon

In silence weave life.
After a while you and I
Will rejoice in the Goddess´ arms
Contemplating the joy of a new spring.
Here on this altar, God the father

and Mother Goddess
Now at this moment when the
night moved to the day
I ask thee to guide my thoughts
To sow in my life seeds of love,
Show me and guide me
towards the road of life.
That the eternal wisdom
is the seed of this time,
That on fertile spirit of Earth
Give me its fruit in my actions and my wishes
And like you God Sun, I will sail to the spirit
On the boat of days.

When the prayer is finished, stand up, and walk barefoot backwards away from the altar. If possible try to hug a tree.

The Esbat

The moon on her month promotes the wizards and witches' meetings, they gather during the different phases in preparation and practice some witching encounters. They can be weekly, biweekly or monthly to practice communitarian rituals to help sowing, harvest, abundance or protection. At this time all the new members are introduced to the group. Their initiation takes place which is done on at the autumn Equinox night, which precedes the Great Sabbat Festival or Akelarre, that corresponds to the fertility ritual.

The hours and their magic

A day has twenty four hours, twelve are sun light, and twelve are darkness. The sunlight hours are divided as follows:

The first sunlight hour at 6:00 a.m., the second at 7:00 a.m., the third one at 8:00 a.m., and so on, until the twelfth sunlight hour reaches 18:00 hours or 6:00 p.m., did you understand?

There are twelve darkness hours which come from 18:00 or 6:00 p.m. until 6:00 a.m., remember this: the first lapse of six hours from 18:00 till 24:00 hours is called Setting and the lapse from 00:00:01until 6:00 a.m. is called Rising.

The first setting hour is at 18:00 or 6:00 p.m., the second one is at 19:00 or 7:00 p.m. and so on until the sixth hour or the last setting hour at 24:00.

The first rising hour is at 1:00 a.m., the second one is at 2:00 a.m. and so on until the sixth rising hour at 6:00 a.m.

Try this:

What time is at the fifth sunlight hour?
What time is at the third setting hour?
What time is at the fourth rising hour?
Congratulations!

You have learned the hours and their magic, the answers are:

The fifth sunlight hour is at 11:00 a.m., the third setting hour is at 21:00 or 9:00 p.m., and the fourth rising hour is at 4:00 a.m.

Witchcraft has some secrets for each group of hours:

Secrets of the rising hours: at the beginning of the day, the rituals that are performed for personal development, and to initiate plans, projects and business, achieving greater power on the new moon phase.

Secrets for the sunlight hours: in the morning, before noon, the mental projection increases, unexpected changes can come at the thirteenth hour or 1 p.m., it´s maybe the strangest time of the sunlight hours, avoid commitments at this time.

Between twelve and one, the cosmic forces seem to stop, they are known as the retrograde hours, when the earth turns around on its own axis gets to a point in which it seems to go back, in ancient times this phenomenon was known as *"The Dancing Sun"*.

Secrets for the setting hours: Towards the sunset, the day forces sleep and the night forces awake. Powerful energies appear and is a key moment to light candles, although it is the death of the day, is the birth of the dark, spirits are wandering around people that suffer, making them more sensitive and unprotected, with increased risk of alterations during the full moon.

The moon has influences on sexuality; gestation of life and abundance. It is who governs fertility.

Secrets for Selene's hours: the moon also has hours during the day in which her force is more favorable depending on the season she is located on (*summer, autumn, fall or spring*). Either way it governs during day or night.

At rising or setting, when the sun births or when it dies. Every day of the week has moments in which the moon exerts more influence.

For Sunday:
- At rising, two in the morning.
- At the fourth sunlight hour or 10 a.m.
- At the eleventh sunlight hour or 5 p.m.
- At setting, 11 p.m.

For Monday:
- At rising, 4 a.m.
- At the first sunlight hour, or 6 a.m.
- At the eighth sunlight hour, or 2 p.m.
- At setting, 8 p.m.

For Tuesday:
- At rising, 3 a.m.
- At the fifth sunlight hour, or 11 a.m.
- At the twelfth sunlight hour, or 6 p.m.
- At setting, or 12 of the night.

For Wednesday:
- At the second sunlight hour, or 7 a.m.
- At the ninth sunlight hour, or 3 p.m.
- At setting, 9 p.m.

For Thursday:
- At rising, 4 a.m.
- At the sixth sunlight hour, or 12 of the day.
- At setting, 6 p.m.

For Friday:
- At rising, 1 a.m.
- At the third sunlight hour, or 9 a.m.
- At the tenth sunlight hour, or 4 p.m.
- At setting, at 10 p.m.

For Saturday:
- At rising, 5 a.m.
- At the seventh sunlight hour, or 1 p.m.
- At setting, 7 p.m.

During these hours it's recommended practicing rituals for gestation and abundance.

The most favorable sunlight hours:
These are the hours during the power of the mind increases, favoring the practice of empowerment rituals or lighting yellow candles to attract balance and home harmony.

For Sunday:
- At the first of sun, or 6 a.m.
- At the seventh sunlight hour.
- At the third setting hour.

For Monday:
- The third rising hour.
- The fourth sunlight hour.
- The eleventh sunlight hour.
- The last setting hour.

For Tuesday:
- The second sunlight hour.
- The eighth sunlight hour.
- The fourth setting hour.

For Wednesday:
- The fourth rising hour.
- The sixth sunlight hour.
- The first setting hour.

For Thursday:
- The third sunlight hour.
- The tenth sunlight hour.
- The fifth setting hour.

For Friday:
- The last rising hour.
- The seventh sunlight hour.
- The second setting hour.

For Saturday:
- The second rising hour.
- The fourth sunlight hour.
- The eleventh sunlight hour.
- The sixth setting hour.

The hours are the same without any variation for the countries with Daylight Saving Time (*DST*).

THE WIZARD'S PROTECTION

Many kinds of parasite energies that could unsettle the mind can come during a ceremony. Let's take some preventive practices to protect yourself.

If you feel assailed by any distressing thoughts during the ritual or memories of deceased relatives come to mind, feel panic, mental absence or confusion, be careful because you have ran into parasite energies; first of all you must be calmed, patient and self-control.

Do not allow them to drag you; avoid desperation, because they might nest in your mind.

There are different physical manifestations of these disturbing presences, the most important are:

Hypothermia

It is reduced environment temperature that causes a strange cold that goes through the body and bones, giving you goose bumps; also with the feeling of being accompanied by invisible but perceptible presences, the candles lights changes and vibrate in a different way

than normal, just like the unusual movement of the mobiles.

If temperature does not regulate in a few minutes, or the environment does not become warm and pleasant, you must finish the ritual. If after a few days the cold temperature continues, you must exorcise the place, there is one or more trapped energies, do not try to practice any magical operation until energetically cleaned.

Tiptology and Raps

These are phsycophonies or incomprehensible voices heard by the mind, just like loud blows or noises causing panic. Sometimes you can hear that someone calls your name, or feeling lightly touched, you also might feel a warm or cold breeze and - numbness of your extremities.

If you hear noises and voices which do not know where they come from, avoid at all costs establishing any kind of communication; if you are called by your name, do not answer; focus on your practice and ignore noises and voices, they may increase for a while to distract you but, if they don't get any attention, it will disappear to never come back.

If you decide to take the risk of establishing contact, it is at your own risk, nobody knows the origin of these kinds of energies. Unless you have knowledge and self-control to dominate the paranormal phenomenon, don't take the risk. Practicing will make you confident, try to record by any electromagnetic media (*audio or video*) your first rituals in order detect any existent sounds (*other than you own*).

Shadows

In semi-darkness, where rituals are practiced, you will see shadows gliding stealthy or dance around you, or a sensation of a body crossing in front of the candles and reflecting itself on the wall. Panic can invade you

and feel a strong impulse to run away because of fear of the unknown.

Never do that. Never abandon a ritual abruptly, your mental health may be at risk; if you practice the steps correctly, specially the recommendations for protection, these rituals should never represent a risk.

During the night, darkness deforms objects transforming them into ghostly shapes, the lights from the candles and the movement of the flames make the shadows seems like moving, giving a strange sensation.

You must be cautious that the place to practice the rituals is free of objects, if it is not possible check which ones project shadows and identify those. In the case of strange shadows that keep their presence, keep in mind that you are in the presence of two-dimensional beings, they won't do anything against you, but will be shadows auguring protection and success to the ritual.

Get used to darkness and feel the protection of shadows, do not flee them, keep your thoughts calmed and stay under control.

Psychic Turbulence

Sometimes, candles go off unexpectedly as if they were blown off by wind from an undefined origin, the things or elements used for the ritual move, the protection circles try to break, and this is due to the powerful energies tuned into your subconscious mind, they have to be exorcised at that moment (*see **exorcism***).

The phenomenon named Poltergeist is very dangerous; it can cause physic and mental damage. Telekinesis phenomenon or object displacement is a product from the mind, it's not a voluntary action, it's very strong energetic influence acting through you. Danger does not consist in the physical damage that it can cause but in the mental disturbance, reaching the point of never knowing whether it is the parasite energy or your own energy. The highest risk is losing your reasoning capacity, and perpetrating violent acts with your thoughts; the psychic disorders become a torture. At night there is a loss of personality, harmony in communal living breaks, and people will never understand; to this date science does not accept these types of psychic disorders.

If you perceive objects moving, stop the ritual and exorcise the place and the objects, this is an unusual phenomenon and rarely appears, but it is important to know how to manage the situation if it happens. It happens in places previously infested, in which many aberrant acts, orgies, crimes, etc. had taken place. Be careful when leaving the place to avoid hurting yourself or others; Is important to stay calmed, remember that desperation is contagious.

Live the experience only if you think that you are a self-confident person, or an investigator of paranormal phenomenon, try to record the event, otherwise, do not attempt the unknown, do not get too impressed, the mind can play tricks on you and it has nothing to do with reality.

Apparitions

Candles are used for every ritual, apparition or ghosts can appear in some of them, it means that there is some kind of energies that condensate to create ectoplasm, mysterious and scary illusions. These apparitions have nothing to do it's just the show of seeing the unknown; they appear, and rapidly fade away. It could happen that the picture remains impregnated in the person's mind to the point of observing the spectrum anywhere involuntarily (*Retinal Persistence*).

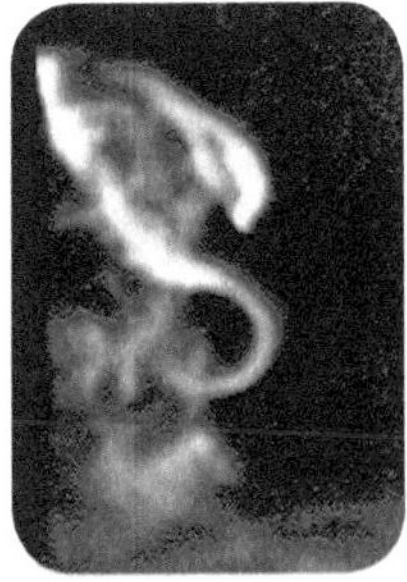

The psychic energies from people already dead can take force and become ectoplasm or an apparition, there is no risk, to the contrary, it is a wonderful experience for the paranormal lovers.

There are two kinds of apparitions:

• *Ectoplasms or Ghosts:* they look like gauze due to the condensation of psychic energy; they are accompanied by hypothermia, raps and flashes of light. The spectrum does not act against people, but sometimes Poltergeist appears.

• *Mental Apparitions:* Although you see a being, it is not real, it's an illusion; unlike the ectoplasms which permit to be filmed or photographed, it is not possible to do it with this kind of apparitions, it does not represent a risk, except the impact that it causes, do not pay attention to them, keep in mind that they are just energies that wander.

Never attempt communication, avoid dialogue with these energies, they actually do not communicate. It is your mind bringing them to life and you suppose that they are talking to you, this will not be more than a mental creation. Never try to mix a ritual of Magick with the practice of Ouija; it is a risk that only depends on you.

Viewers

The place gets impregnated by pleasant and/or unpleasant smells and sounds, giving the feeling that you are not alone in the room, that there is someone else there; those are announcements of presences of parasite energies which are attracted by the ritual that is being practiced at that time.

Sometimes those presences become annoying and unpleasant, sometimes disturbing, don't worry, they will go away soon, although they leave behind some smells some pleasant, others very uncomfortable.

To avoid this situation, keep seven different flowers in the room to perfume the environment before you start any ritual, as well as an alive being which is known in Magick as *"the bank"* or *"Protector"*, it can be a bird, a fish, a cat, etc. It is necessary to remember certain predispositions to get started in the world of magic, such as:

• **Peace of Mind:** Serenity is a virtue that must be trained day after day in order to control the mind in the case of being involved in an unexpected difficulty. Handle the fear and dread when beginning the practice of any ritual, never assume anything. Avoid revenge, hate thoughts and feelings in your daily living. Remember, during the practice feelings attract - energies that vibrate in the same scale. If you feel hate, will attract hate, if you feel love, will attract love.

• **Concentration:** By having your mind under control, you prevent it from running into panic. The lack of concentration and serenity causes us to make the wrong decisions. You are going to carry out a ritual of Magick not a game, your mind must be concentrated, otherwise, you can be blocked by distraction, resulting in a blockage in the energies and it can refuse to work for your rituals. The unnecessary foolishness closes the gates of knowledge.

• **Physical Control:** There are some magic acts that demand concentration and physical stillness for long lapses of time; for example, to save a sick person you might need several days, that's why you need to cultivate the mental and physical discipline by strengthening the will. Remember that exercising is a great alternative. Self-control is prudent and learn how master physical tiredness produced by the fact of staying in one position for a long periods of time; magic does not require sacrifices, rituals can be done without stiffness, if you need to move, do it. Be careful about staying inside the protection circle, because your physical being is not as important as that of the concentrated mind.

• **Sleep Management:** The most magical activities are practiced at night, and one of the most difficult-thing to do is to control - sleepiness. Keep in mind how dangerous it can be -working at night- using fire. Lack of sleep and fatigue can put you to -sleep, you could be trapped by energies, it could start a fire. If you are tired, get some rest, do not force yourself. Anxiety is not a partner of magic.

Before you start keep in mind the following:

• Forget about prejudices and dogmas.
• Study carefully each part.
• Start your reading and practice.

• Witchcraft is the art of applying wisdom to find harmony with nature.

Start practicing and you will notice immediate changes in your life. Can we do a text?

I invite you to stop reading right now. Get some cinnamon sticks and place them under your house doors, leave them there for seven days and evaluate the changes obtained. Magic!

Discover the unlimited power latent in your mind; everything as a "*whole*" lives within you, and you can create countless alternatives for your own life if want to; make the decision to be yourself. Become a wizard or a witch, taking control of nature's elements and spirits, creating your own universe.

Do not hesitate! There is unlimited knowledge within you, let it flow; take actions to make your destiny ruled by your mind instead of having a life ruled by the circumstances. The knowledge of nature and its secrets will open doors never imagined. You will be the master of the world.

CHAPTER III

THE ALCHEMICAL WORK

«We own nothing, but we can own it all»

The Alchemy is an ancient Arabic word that means *"the transmutation of the ordinary into something valuable"*. The wizard, by applying the great power of witchcraft makes mental transmutation, dominating the laws of nature, finding balance between the superior and the inferior, and fatuous with eternal, disclosing the elixir of life; Alchemy is a mental art.

Witchcraft and the magical arts, initially require a place to do the rituals, counting on the necessary tools for the preparation of potions and other tasks. This place is known as The Covent, it has to be inscrutable and secret; here is where the wizard or witch does their great work, transmuting matters and thoughts assisted by the angel's forces, the power of the elements and the mental magic.

Only with practice and experience is possible to arrive at the point of transforming this elements initially physical, into mental projections, meaning that, after

some time, you will not need anything material other than the power of your concentration to do a ritual; creating your own mental Covent, and becoming a powerful wizard or witch. Build an altar in your Covent, with simple and modest non-valuable objects; the humbler the elements are, more will be the power of the magic. The wizard or witch tools are:

Altar: It could be a big discrete table, able to work with four people, better if it is round, symbol of equality and non-hierarchical. It is the gateway to the world of angels, to another different dimension. So keep it clean, perfumed and harmonized. You can build it inside the house, outdoors, close to a tree or near a river.

Draw a five-pointed star; be careful of the location, the pentagram with one upward point means protection, with two, destruction. Use five stones (*collected in the river*) of different colors, set them on the five points, in the center of the star, place essences and objects that you want to magnetize. According to the season you are in, direct the tip of the star to face:

• To the north in the summer, Fire element.
• To the east in the fall, Air element.

- To the south in the winter, Water element.
- To the west in the spring, Earth element.

Always do the rituals at the altar, protected by the circles, added to the invocations; the presence of angels and spirits will empower the enchantment.

At the altar it is necessary to have representations of the four elements:

- Fire: Candles, yellow flowers
- Earth: Stones, sand, plants
- Wind: Essences, perfumes, aromas, incenses, ink and inkwell.
- Water: Oils, water, sap, blood.

Place a devise that produces pleasant sounds close to the table; it will be of grand help preventing presence of energies. In the same way, keep colored wooden pins dispersed around the table, they are a great protection.

The Star of Solomon: On a wall or piece of fabric draw the Star of Solomon, and two overlapped triangles, symbol of wisdom, which are related to the seven Hermetic Principles; to keep them in mind while practicing the magical arts:

• **Mentalism:** The universe and all that exists is mind; it is a constant thought in the infinite mind of everything as a whole.

• **Correspondence:** The power is the same; both, top and bottom, in the mind of the whole or in the mind of every being. Big and small differ only in the point of view.

• **Vibration:** Stillness does not exist; everything is in constant movement, the mental vibrations join the absolute vibration of everything as a whole.

• **Polarity:** Nothing exists in the universe without its complement. They are not opposites, but the opposite of the same. For example: love and hate are the opposite side of feelings, and the one is the complements of the other.

• **Rhythm:** Mutation in life, comes and goes, it is birth and death, the consent and the decline, it is the return of the advance, going and returning.

• **Causation:** The events of life, even if they seem strange, they never occur by chance, on the contrary, the laws which rule the universe produce the necessary causes to make something happen. You have this book in your hands due to countless causes but not by chance.

• **Generation:** The mind gestates taking the strength of the first causation; it is the constant rebirth of the same energy by infinite, different ways transmuted by the power of the thought.

• **Tablecloth:** We use two tablecloths, a white one and a black one sewn together: draw a red circle on each side of the tablecloths as a symbol of equilibrium, leave space enough in the middle to set the pentagram and the compass. You also may have your tools within the tablecloth to keep them protected from curious people.

• **Book of Shadows:** It's the wizard or witch's diary, it must be handwritten, using a language understandable only for the owner; it is used to express achievements, techniques and discoveries to preserve the knowledge in order to transmit it to new generations, thanks to the existence of these books, much information outlasted until the current days.

• **Wardrobe:** Skin is the best dress, if it's hard for you to be naked, use comfortable clothing, being careful with the sleeves considering that you will work with fire. Do not use bright clothing because it produces distracting sparkles; do not use underwear either, because nature doesn't need to be covered.

• **Candles:** These are the most important objects to practice magical rituals; they are representation of light and protection. Normally, we use candles of different colors; it depends on the ritual we want to practice relating color with petition, for that reason it's important to remember the four colors belonging to the four Elements. (*Find combinations and rituals with candles in the book* **"The Magic of Candles"**). When lighting a candle, cross it with your hands by moving them on circles over, the ancient Wiccan magic teaches how to write the initials of your name on the air rounding the candle before lighting it to make it more powerful.

• **Chandeliers:** they normally have an odd number of arms, three or seven, they are made of bronze, it is recommended to get a new one, if they are antique may are infested of energies; the best ones are those made by yourself. Abstain yourself from using old chandeliers to do rituals, that could release psychic disturbances. Use your chandeliers to light the room. Do not use them at the altar.

• **Candle holders:** They are used to put the candles and avoid a conflagration; it's recommended finding black candle holders, with a wide base to gather up the wax. In the event of candle holders of different color are used, they must be of the same color of the candle, and must also be used at the altar.

• **Candle snuffer:** The most convenient snuffers for rituals have a wooden stick and a metallic bell. Do not buy antiquities, you could run the risk of being infested by energies, don't blow candles to put them out, instead of it extinguish the flame using the candle snuffer to maintain them irradiated with energy.

• **Thurible:** it is the crucible to burn incenses, you can also use a cauldron with an extra support to put beneath a candle to heat it up.

• **Other objects:** A clay jar with water, a big crystal recipient that works as an aquarium to have a fish you must take care of, a moon mirror that is easy to handle, white, red, yellow and black chalks to draw the protection circles, a mortar to mix several ingredients, small bottles, wooden boxes to keep preparations, oils and mixtures, make a small herbarium to keep dry herbs and flowers.

In as much as your knowledge and experience in magical arts increase, you will acquire some more tools, Magick uses varieties of things such as a pin and a mountain. There are many treatises about plants and stones which will be a great help for you, don't forget that Wicca is a synonym of knowledge.

SECRETS FOR THE PREPARATION OF MAGICAL PRODUCTS

The power of the mind irradiates and captures psychical energy in the objects that manipulates, such objects are governed by the law of similarity becoming in turn into vehicles to transmit enchantments or witchcraft to accomplish the work they were created for.

At unifying with a person or a wish, those objects release the wizard or witch's energy to be imposed during the rituals. Every object increases and engenders is similar that flows through prayers and invocations, capturing the wish in the corresponding Element and Elemental.

It does not exist a list of magic and witchcraft products, the apprentice has to know that it is the owner of a

creator and powerful mind which gives him/her the four powers to complement the witchcraft.

Hereafter, we'll give you a list as an example to prepare some products, you must know that in magical arts it is possible to use many kinds of ingredients such as a sand particle or a star; it is the mind of the wizard or witch who gives life to the products through rituals.

• Fire Element

• **Fire Sand:** You must use seven dry sweet plants, seven dry bitter plants and dry wood, mix the ingredients and put them on fire until they become into white ashes during a New Moon night; later, grid the mixture in the mortar while repeating the following spell at least fifteen times until you have finished:

This Earth
I (say your name) am burning
With powers will be
Enchanted forever
To the magic of loving
My spell will go in effect!
With the fire sand will be done!

With salamanders and magical beings
My thoughts will come true!

It is recommended to prepare a quantity enough to be used in other rituals.

• **Magnetized Candles:** Before practicing a ritual is important to unify yourself with candles, it is not required to do it every time, you may have a considerable quantity of magnetized candles to light at the same time with the ones which in turn will get impregnated with those energies to use them in a magical practice.

The magnetization must be done under the influence of the New Moon; take ten yellow candles, put them on the altar, light them with the pentagram point facing to the north, get your hands close to the candles and invoke the Fire element, let your energies flow, and looking at the flames say:

The Four Corners of the Earth

For the guardians of the four points:
Seraph, Cherub, Tharsis and Ariel
Princes of the Elements,

I (say your name) invoke you
At this solemn time
And in the presence of this altar
Made for you
I call on you to give your power
To these candles
And make that their flames
transport the influence
Of my wishes to come true
By your intercession.

*(Recite the invocation to the Fire Element from the book "**Alchemy**")*

When finished, put off the candles and keep them in a place where they don't get in contact to sunlight, cover them with a black cloth.

Every time you use one or more candles for a magical practice, light them with one of the magnetized ones, that way, the new candles will get magnetized too; you will need to do the ritual again as soon as they run out.

• Earth Element

Cauldron of the Magical beings: Put in a clay pot some petals from different yellow flowers, seven different kinds of soil such as lime, sand, soil from a ground, clay, salt, river stones, soil from a hill, etc.; in a waning moon night invoke the Earth Element setting seven black candles around the altar, after that pulverize the content of the clay pot including it, and let that mixture weathering on a mirror; the preparation must receive the influence of the sun and the moon. In the case of adding some cemetery soil as an extra ingredient and making the respective spell, you will have as a result a witchcraft product known as Flying Powder that is used to dispel undesirable people, bad neighbors, and third persons who get involved in other's relationships.

• **Magic Stones:** Get three river stones and put them on a place to receive sunlight for about three days, avoiding that they receive moonlight. Then, put them all between two mirrors to make them get the infinite's forces. Conjure them with the Invocation of the Magical Beings and Undines.

• **Abundance Seeds:** They are representation of prosperity, they belong to Earth and Air Elements; fall transports the seeds to turn green again in the spring, maintaining the harmony of the cycles.

Get some seeds of different fruits; place them out in the open to receive the influence of the moon. The color of the seed you decide to use depends on the ritual you want to practice, according to the following items:

• **To get material abundance:** waning moon; brown, green and yellow fruits.

• **To get your new plans:** waxing moon; red and black fruits (*grapes*).

• **To get your goals:** new moon; yellow and orange fruits.

• **To find love:** full moon; green, red and yellow fruits.

Put the seed on a mirror at the altar; get your hands close to them to irradiate with your wish, it is recommended to magnetize the seed after having sexual relations.

• **Sweet and Bitter Plants:** they are used to prepare baths, watering, exorcisms and rituals; the bitter plants work for cleaning and protecting and the sweet ones work to increase and maintain prosperity.

Keeping in mind that flora changes depending on the region of the world, they can be replaced with plants possible to find where you live.

Bitter Plants: wormwood, white poplar, birch, hemlock, ruta, purple and black basil, dandelion, etc. *Sweet Plants:* Cinnamon, mint, anise, cedron, chamomile, clove, blossom, etc.

Let them dry overshadowed, as well as they are dehydrated, pulverize them in the mortar and pack them in white bags or in bottles. Plants don't need to be magnetized with an additional ritual but just at the moment of making a magical operation.

• **Amber Oil:** In a waning moon night, at the first setting hour, working at the altar, fill a transparent bottle with a quarter of mineral oil and a quarter of water, add three drops of sandal essence and introduce an amber seed; recite the invocation of The Four Corners of the Earth and the Invocation of the Element.

Earth:

For the guardians of the four points
Seraph, Cherub, Tharsis and Ariel
Princes of the Elements,
I (*say your name*) invoke you
At this solemn time
And in the presence of this altar made for you
I call on you to give power
To this preparation
And make that its seed gestate
my wishes to come true
By your intercession.

*(Recite the invocation of the Earth Element from the book "**Alchemy**").*

Let your ritual under moon influence and pick it up at the last rising time before getting in contact to the sunlight. Keep it in a safe and protected place.

• Air Element

While preparing perfumes, recite at the altar the following invocation:

For the guardians of the four points
Seraph, Cherub, Tharsis and Ariel
Princes of the Elements,
I (say your name) invoke you
At this solemn time
And in the presence of this altar made for you
I call on you to give power
To these perfumes and essences
And make that their smells
transport the influence
Of my wishes to come true
By your intercession.

(Recite the invocation to the Air Element from the book **"Alchemy"***)*

• **Oil of Love:** In the first-quarter phase, put 2 ounces of pure mineral oil (*odorless, flavorless, and colorless*) in a bottle, add some cinnamon sticks and petals from 7 red flowers, put these objects under the moon influence for three consecutive nights; at the fourth day, strain the preparation on the altar to get a clean oil, put the oil in a dark bottle while reciting the invocation of The Four Corners of the Earth. If your wish is to attract someone special, put an object that belongs to that person.

• **Perfume of Stars:** Collect petals from 10 daisies and put them under sunlight for seven days to dry. Pulverize and then mix them in a liter of hot water (*as an infusion*). Let the preparation settle until it gets cold and then put it out in the open for seven nights to be influenced by the Full Moon.

• **Fall Fragrance:** In a full moon night, at the rising hours, put a liter of water under moon influence; add some cinnamon sticks, orange peels and petals of three white flowers. Put the preparation out under sunlight for one day, after that put it on the altar for nine days, then strain it while reciting the invocation of The Four Corners of the Earth; keep it in a fresh place.

• **Venus and Mars Perfume:** You must prepare the same formula on Friday for Venus and on Tuesday for Mars. Take a bottle with water and mix it with seven wild flowers, all of them picked up on Sunday at the first sun hour. Dig fifteen centimeters and take five stones from a virgin place (*a mountain, a valley, etc.*), put them on fire until getting hot, be careful of burning yourself; put the stones in the bottle that contains the flowers, do this on the altar; put a lid on the bottle and conjure it with the Four Corners of the Earth invocation. This perfume is used in Love rituals.

• Water Element

Recite the following invocation while preparing products related to this Element:

The Four Corners of the Earth

For the guardians of the four points
Seraph, Cherub, Tharsis and Ariel
Princes of the Elements,
I (say your name) invoke you
At this solemn time
And in the presence of this altar made for you
I call on you to give power to this water
That represents the blood of life
And gestate my wishes to come true
By your intercession.

(Recite the invocation of the Water Element).

• **Conjured Oil:** Put some drops of Sandal essence and some cinnamon sticks in an ounce of mineral oil. Put it out to receive the New Moon's influence for the seven days of the entire phase, being very careful of avoiding the preparation to get in contact with sunlight.

• **Moon's Water:** Get four transparent and clean bottles which you will tag according to the phase of the moon when the water was collected. In the first New Moon night, you will collect the first bottle of water; the second bottle will be collected in a waxing moon, the third one is the Full Moon's bottle, and finally you will collect the waning moon's bottle. They have to be placed out in the open to receive moonlight as well as sunlight. Put the four bottles on the altar, at the four corners; put your hands close to them one by one to irradiate with your personal energy while reciting the invocation of The Four Corners of the Earth for the Water Element. Keep them in a dark place. Remember that everything decreases in the waning moon, growing and development initiate in the New Moon, everything is stimulated in the waxing moon, and the goals are reached in the Full Moon.

• **Energy Channelizer:** Put a liter of water in a transparent bottle, add seven sweet plants at the first setting hours in a Full Moon, let the preparation out in the open for one night to be influenced by the moon as well as during the next day to receive power from the sun; the following night, put the bottle in the middle of the altar and recite the invocation of The Four Corners of the Earth while passing your hands over the bottle. Keep it in a safe place.

Exorcisms

A ritual of magic is an intention that comes from the mind with a strong wish of doing well; therefore, psychic energies of protection released to avoid and cleaning the existent ones.

During an exorcism, the released energies will influence the emotional state, generating some changes of behavior; illusions come up and cause confusion. If you are completely focused on what you are doing, nothing can alter anything. Repeat the prayers at the same time of invoking the Spirits of the Elementals (*the four prayers of the Four Cardinal Points*).

While practicing all the exorcisms, recite:

*I (say your name) exorcise you
Oh! Creature of the... (Say the Element of the creature:
Water, Earth, Air, or Fire)
To get away from you all the impurities
And residues of the material world.*

*I exorcise you in the name of
the Goddess Mother Diana
And God the Father Faun.*

Cleaning: Exorcise the place, it is not about building a temple, the simpler the operations the bigger the benefit you will obtain, presumptuousness and luxury chase away the angels inspiring negative thoughts, envy and rivalry from other people.

Conjuring to exorcise the place:

*Aeterne sapiens, fortis, potens,
Ens Entium Creator mundi
Veni in hunc Locum,
Et tua presentia majestate sanctificia
Hunc locum ut meo sit puritas Castitas
Et plenitude legis,*

Et sicus fumus incense
istius ad te ascendit,
Sic in hunc locum descendant virtus tua
Et benediction tua et vos omnes angeli
Et spiritus omnes hunc consecration
Adstate

Presents per deum verum,
Vivum et aeternum qui vos sicut et me
Ex nihilo creative
Et qui vos simul sicut nos uno momento
Destricere potest et per sapientiam ejus.
Amen.

• Exorcism of Clothing:

Clothing for daily use gets impregnated with static energies, for example, shiny silk and wood because they glint at night. Clothing also gets impregnated with energies of people around you, perfumes and corporal smells. The best dress to do rituals is the skin; you may also wear a clean loose-fitting cloth and your body must be clean too in order to accomplish the appointment with the Elements and Angels.

Pronounce the following conjuring in the presence of the clothing you will wear:

O pater conditor alme siderum sapientia
Summa per omnes fortitudines
tuus et virtutes
Tuas sanctificare digneris
Vestem hanc Tuo honori
Preparatam Exorciso te vestis per
Deum verum.
Vivum aeternum qui cuncta
fecit ex nihilo et mehi
Sit in hoc meo opere quod sit impurum
Sed virtutis plenum.
Amen.

• Exorcism of the Book:

It is used to unify the book with you; you will find prayers and invocations practiced for many years for those who had connection with the Elements; with it, the doors of wisdom are open to find the path to a parallel world full of Angels. The book, as such, is just used to get information, discovering the real content is an art; it is a constant practice to change the life of the person who discovers the enclosed power. If you put in practice such comments and lessons, you will get happiness.

Consecration of the Book:

Hel, ye, Eye, ye princeps principium,
Ens entium, miserere mei et respice in
Me servum tuum N. Qui te devotissime
Invocat et te per nomen tuum sanctissimum
Tremendum. Tetragramaton supplicat
Ut sis propicius et felix mihi in

Opertionibus meis et jubeas angelis
Et spiritibus tuis venire et sedem in hoc
Loco ponere. O vos omnes angeli spiritus
Stellarum, o vos omnes angeli spiritus
Elementorum, ó vos omnes spiritibus
Adstantes ante faciem dei conjurat vos
Minister et servus fidelis altissimi conjurat
Vos deus ens entium o tetragramaton, ut
Nunc et nunc veniatis et adsistatis huic
Operationi. Venite orat vos et supplicat
Humilissime servus dei.
Amen.

• Exorcism of the tools:

The objects necessary to practice magical and divinatory arts must be conjured to irradiate them with your personal energy. It is recommended to practice this ritual at the rising hours on Sunday. To do it, light some black candles, the room has to be completely dark.

These tools are going to be only yours and the humblest they are the best energy will flow from them. Abstain yourself from using them for any other task, do not lend them or allow other people to get in contact with them.

Conjuration of the tools:

Aeterne sapiens, fortis, potens,
Ens Entium Creator mundi veni in hunc
Locum, et tua presentia majestate
sanctificia hunc locum ut meo sit
Puritas Castitas et plenitude legis,
Et sicus fumus incensi
Istius ad te ascendit, sic in hunc
locum descendant virtus tua
Et benediction tua et vos omnes angeli
Et spititus omnes hunc consecration
adstate presents per deum verum,

Vivum et aeternum qui
Vos sicut et me ex nihilo creativ
Et qui vos simul sicut nos uno momento
Destricere potest et per sapentiam ejus,
Amen.

Circles of Protection

Before starting a ritual is essential to comply with some provisions of protection to take care of yourself from the events that happen at practicing rituals to take you off guard. Certain energies are invoked and evoked during rituals, therefore, even if the reading has been well done, some of those unknown energies would catch you when you least expect it, taking you to live an experience full of panic; that's the reason why the objects of protection are needed.

How to make them:

Draw three circles around the altar. Make them with some different materials, lime, sand, chalk. The best material is Fire Sand.

• **First Circle of Protection (external):** At starting the ritual draw a circle counterclockwise with the elements, managing a prudent distance taking into account that you must draw two more circles. This is called *"Circle of External Protection"*.

• Second Circle of Protection (middle): Draw it clockwise at ten centimeters from the first circle, there mustn't be any object between the two circles and be careful of drawing this circle with double the thickness of the external one. Avoid any weakness on the lines; the line of this circle is perpetual or continuous, especially because this circle is the most protective against parasite energies.

• Third Circle of Protection (internal): Draw half circle clockwise and half circle counterclockwise; the altar, you and the tools have to be in the middle of the three circles. There must be space enough into the circles to loosely move.

To easily draw the circles, use a cord tied to something heavy at one end and a glass or jar within the object to mark at the other end; at having defined the measurement of each circle, draw them continuous and wide closed at the ends. Make them slowly and carefully, don't repeat them, be focused and mentally clean.

After making the circles don't get out from them for any reason, at least that your life is in danger, otherwise, wait in the circles until finishing the rituals and close the door to the dimension of energies. Circles must be erased in the same direction they were drawn; pick up carefully the objects you used and put them in bags very respectfully. Do not break or step over the circles!

It's important to consider that the point of union of the line is the same point to conclude the ritual, it means that the closing point to erase the circles of protection has to be the same opening point.

Conjuration of the circles, after drawing them:

I *(say your name)* conjure you
Circles of Protection
You are the border between the world of men
And the kingdom of powerful Angels.
I invoke the guardians
Of the north, Of the east
Of the south, Of the west
To be my protection.
I consecrate you
Oh, Circles of Power!

INVOCATIONS AND EVOCATIONS

While the mind is in trance it is sensitive and susceptible of being possessed; there is a sort of communication during rituals with the Elements which flow through the candles and the magnetized objects.

There is a risk of infestation at saying conjurations and invocations, protect yourself; you are in the presence of unknown energies which can seriously damage your mental and physical health. These psychic energies are known as spirits and angels of people who have practiced magical arts for many years; every person who practices a ritual invoking certain energy increases the personal power like an inverse pyramid to the infinite. They were initiated with the creation of life and will be nourished day after day by those who are unified with them.

Keep in mind the items before practicing a ritual:

• The Circles of Protection
• Tranquility and mental training
• Foolproof determination
• Conviction and peace.

Invoking is the action of attracting energies from angels and spirits though prayers and magic formulas in order to get protection, support and help to become a purpose reality. A physical manifestation could or couldn't exist, sometimes they appear like dreams or though inexplicable events. At practicing an invocation you won't see the spectacular apparitions invented by fantasy (*or those apparitions watched on movies and TV*); in case of practicing invocations with negative intentions, the angels will leave and will be difficult to contact them again.

Invocations must be pronounced aloud or like a mental projection, the origin of these energies is psychical, and the intention has to be talking to them. Communication is established through your thoughts thanks to a great concentration, so you will strike up a conversation with the invoked angels; they won't be in your life as people or advisors, they will be present in specific situations. Their mission is to protect life and combining the ties to become your wishes reality; sometimes happens that their answers come represented by events apparently adverse. For example, losing your job to get a better one, delaying to be in a meeting which saves you from an accident. They don't work based on our whishes but in using their wisdom to face adverse situations.

There are angels of the Elements and angels of beings and species, they were known by the indigenous as *"The spirit of Nature"* or *"The Great Manitou"*.

At the moment of invoking angels and spirits, energies of dead people are present allowing the evocation; this is a risky art for people who decide adventure without knowledge or preventive measures. People, who appeal to it, are looking for a benefit acquired from destruction using dead people's energies.

Spirits denominated *"unclean"*, are easily misled with angels and we don't know how to identify them; when invoking energies of the Elements, they don't appear physically because their energy works silently. On the contrary, when evoking spirits, they make a physical presence with a personal identity, rejecting orders from the wizard or the evoker and taking over the place where they were evoked; it is required to practice an exorcism to get them free.

They adopt any form or shape; they also use the image of known dead people, with the purpose of confusing the evoker. They are shapeless energies and their physical presence is a projection from our mind.

*The Master **Kadaisha** said:*

«Remember that good doesn't exist for evil; evil takes the shape of good to commit evil».

The use of Ouija Board is popular, it is sold for stores as an innocent toy, but it hides evil inside. You may connect with destruction by evoking the presence of energy, and the session begins. Ouija invites you to use it many times and at different hours creating dependence. Danger begins at getting information about future events and creating a feeling of superiority to the person who practices it; wishes come true to make the person believe that the evocation has had an answer.

Your life starts changing and your ignorance makes you think that is beneficial for you, barriers are broken and the advance is immediate; you don't realize that temporary tricks have trapped you. The evoked energies are charging a high price, your goals are annulled and you go to supposed «*saviors*».

Goetia just nested and there is nothing to do, you will join those who walk through evil; if you play with Ouija and make an evocation, the energies of a dead being are always present and make you believe that they are the person you evoked, but, how do you do to be sure about the identity of that presence? We recommend avoiding practicing evocative arts if you don't know the protection techniques, and even knowing them, you should think if it is worthwhile. In case of choosing that option, remember that you will never scape from that influence.

*The Master **Kadaisha** said:*

«Evil wears a thousand masks, and maybe the most dangerous of them hides into apparent innocence».

An old story tells better this experience. We invite you to read the story of Faust, written by the German writer Johann Wolfgang Von Göethe; Faust sold his soul to evil due to his ambition for material things; finally he lost everything including himself.

Now you know the risks, you are already prepared for initiating invocations, ready to do the circles of protection; the angels will work on avoiding the presence of parasite energies.

Recite the following invocations of protection every time you make a new ritual. Don't forget to put the point of the pentagram drawn on the altar towards the cardinal point according to the current season.

Put four candles (*green, red, yellow and blue*) on their corresponding candle holders, shaping a rhombus; light them before reciting the prayers.

Place them this way:

• To the North, summer, among June, July and August; Fire Element. A red candle.
• To the East, fall, among September, October and November; Air Element. A white candle.

• To the South, winter, among December, January and February; Water Element. A blue candle.

• To the West, spring, among March, April and May; Earth Element. A black candle.

Looking at the North, recite:

Oh, angels of the night!
Salamanders of Fire and light
Purify this space,
And protect my skin,
During this magical operation
Which I undertake at this hour
With your benevolence.

Looking at the East, recite:

Oh, angels of the night!
Sylphs and Sylphids of the Air
Purify this space,
And protect my thoughts,
During this magical operation
Which I undertake at this hour
With your benevolence.

Looking at the South, recite:

Oh, angels of the night!
Undines of the Water
Purify this space,
And protect my blood,
During this magical operation
Which I undertake at this hour
With your benevolence.

Looking at the West, recite:

Oh, angels of the night!
Magical beings and Gnomes of the Earth
Purify this space,
And protect my body,
During this magical operation
Which I undertake at this hour
With your benevolence.

SORTILEGES, FILTERS, SPELLS AND ENCHANTMENTS

The power of witchcraft concentrates through conjurations, capturing such power in different potions wherewith the wizard or witch concludes the great work that is materializing thoughts.

Filters and sortileges are magnetized separately to be used during the rituals, whether it is an object, it must be kept in a dark colored bag; whether it is a perfume, it must be applied on the body at the rising hours.

Spells and enchantments have as a fundament the power of the word and sight, the charmer magnetizes by his/her presence.

The hands are important, keep them perfectly well-presented, take care of them, you will enchant and practice rituals with them.

I personally prefer wearing black, it increases energy. Wearing this color is not a craving, it has a condition: the mystery that identifies a wizard or witch, he/she irradiates a charisma different than normal, he/she knows that an act of love, helping someone, feeding someone, listening without speaking, not discussing, a clean vocabulary, and all those simple acts that create in his/her mind the philosophy of life are the secret of power.

Always keep your practices in secret; if someone discovers you, it has to be because of your acts but never because of your words. Exercise your body daily, so you will be very good looking, attraction is the beginning of enchantment. Speak slowly; practice a meditation technique, yoga would be excellent; the great Master who sleeps inside of you will awake to become you into a guide to the others.

At the moment of harmonizing your mind, body and spirit, you will enchant just using your sight and your words; you will get the point of making something reality only wishing it.

*The Master **Kadaisha** said:*

"*Think well what you wish because you will get it, and could happen if you obtain it, that you won't want it anymore.*
***If you get it, you can't dispel it*"**

Filter:

Aromas, perfumes and scents belong to the Air Element; they are verb and thoughts, movements, incense and dancing. Their force depends on the operator's mind to magnetize them.

In a Full Moon night, take the object (*perfume, writing, pin, picture, cigar, etc.*) you want to irradiate with your energy, put it on a mirror that reflexes the moonlight, and focusing your mind get your hands close to it without touching, imagine what you want to obtain of the ritual.

Use the verb to decree your desire, and imperatively order:

For the power of the Elements,
I command you to:
Become into reality (say your wish)

If the conjuration is to ask for something to the future, to advance or progress, move the objects onwards, showing them the direction; if the conjuration is to forget something or someone or to separate, move them backwards; if the conjuration is to get a job or goals, move the objects clockwise; if the conjuration is to avoid the presence of evil energies, move the objects counterclockwise.

Filters must be sweet if you want them to increase a feeling and bitter to generate an attraction; remember that your thoughts at the moment of practicing the ritual will impregnate the object.

Preparation of a Love Filter:

You will need:

- Mineral oil
- Seven yellow flowers
- Seven petals of red rose
- Cinnamon and sandal
- A white feather
- Orange peels

Take each ingredient separately and start practicing the ritual of love, if possible, with an object or picture.

Place all the ingredients in front of a mirror and proceed:

Mix cinnamon with sandal in a bowl, put the flowers, petals and orange peels in, pour the oil while mixing with the feather. Think of the person, and while preparing the filter say aloud:

Make him/her feel, make him/her feel
That I love him/her in his/her absence.
Make him/her come, make him/her come
And nothing can stop him/her.

Mine is the love
Mine is the magic
Today and forever
Mine is the illusion.

The perfume is now *"charged with the magic of love"*, put the preparation in a transparent bottle, put it on your skin daily, and if possible rub it on the person you desire, use only a drop to avoid being perceived; he or she will feel strongly drawn.

Well then, you can lead the way of preparing your own perfumes; remember that the Air Element is everything that transports thoughts.

Sortileges

Sortileges must be done in the waning moon nights when the moon loses its force, it is a moment to attract abundance (*of money, love and health*); the operations practiced during the waning moon gradually gain power while the moon runs to the New Moon phase, getting stronger at waxing moon and finally coming true at full moon.

Use gold objects, bitter plants, seeds of green fruits and river stones collected by you in a waning moon night, these stones are known as *"Altar Stones"*.

Plants, flowers, herbs, stones and gems are parts of a sortilege; it would be a great help for you to get a four-leaf clover in a Full Moon night.

Let's make an abundance sortilege, in a waning moon night, at the first rising hour.

You will need:

- Fire sand
- 7 orange seeds
- 7 sweet plants
- One lemon
- 4 big headed pins
- 4 white flowers
- 4 yellow flowers
- 2 black candles
- A bowl with water enough to take a bath
- One white bag

Procedure:

With your altar ready to work on, follow the instructions:

Invocation of the Nature's Spirits

Small beings from anywhere…
(Read A*ttraction of Good Luck*)

Light two black candles on the side of the altar.

Take the lemon, while putting the pins in it, pointing to the four points, invoke the Angels of the four cardinal points (*read the section: Invocations and Evocations*); then, put the lemon on the table.

Strip the leaves off the seven plants, let them drop in the bowl with water, and carefully put the eight flowers floating on the water. Dust the fire sand over the bowl while pronouncing your wish:

For the power of the Fire, for the power of the Water, make mi wish, to greatly increase.

For the power of the Air, for the power of the Earth, that this sortilege, bring money to me.

Wet the orange seeds in the water and put them in the white bag. Finish the ritual.

Next morning, simmer the preparation avoiding that the water boils, afterwards, wash up the house with this infusion and take a shower with the rest of the water.

Take the plants, flowers, seeds and lemon to bury them in a flowerpot. The next first-quarter phase you will see amazing results.

Spells and Enchantments

Spells and Enchantments are very common in magical practices, they contain the force of the thoughts; a sight, a word, a sentence, have the power to bewitch and enchant.

Every magical ritual without exceptions must contain a spell or enchantment, created by you according to your desire.

Enchantments are rhymes to transport a wish transmitted by the power of the word or by rounds with the message. To create the rounds, use the name of the person, the hair color, etc.

They can be done changing the order of the syllables by threes in threes or the number you prefer; this way, only you will know the meaning of the pronounced enchantment; for example:

The morning sun
When the moon shines
Your soul will be mine...

We must start counting the syllables in order of threes in threes, starting at the first syllable (*The*), and counting the rest of them in the same order, without repeating a syllable until finishing all of them. You will obtain as a result, the same text but written as follows:

Ning the nes
Sun shi be
Mor you're the soul
Moon mi when...

By pronouncing these words, the spell will be powerful. As you practice this technique, you will find many combinations to create your own spells. Write them in the Book of the Shadows.

Remember that a spell can't be undone, it will return increased to you according to the number you use to write it, if it's 3, multiply 3 times what you will receive.

The enchanter irradiates a special magnetism through his or her wearing style, the way of walking and speaking projected by his or her look, movements and words using rhymes; for example, fixedly looking at what you want, say:

You will be mine, before the clock strikes nine Everywhere and anywhere, wherever you will go, my spell will go with you so.

Use it to enchant objects or people.

Practice this experience to train yourself in the art of spells and enchantments:

Put the palms of your hands close but not together, with no more than two centimeters between them, feel the air flowing in your fingers. Focus on feeling… move the hands softly, as if you had an imaginary ball between them. Perceive for a few minutes, fine! You perceive your energy field and your personal magnetism, increase it freely! You will be without a doubt a great wizard or witch. Now, release your hands and feel the energy running by your body; to the extent that you let it flow, your aura will grow, and if you have a constant and disciplined training, will heal with your hands just in three months.

Use this spells to materialize your wishes:

In your room or your place, build an altar
A candle, a jar and a mirror, you will have to
enchant.

Fire, Earth, Air and Water, only one they are
Silent and using them a gift you will find.

Every letter that you write, with a black feather
you'll blow, those who get them in their hands
By enchantment will love you.

Using what you want and thinking of your desire, is
possible to enchant
Putting it on the altar and saying a prayer.
Wear a necklace to attract love

Look in a mirror his or her reflect
His or her name thirteen, times you will say aloud
and to make real this spell yet,
He or she you will reject.
If you want to be enchanting
Be whatever you imagine to be.
At each corner put one, complete
the circle without fear, four are the candles,
They will give you the gift.

If someone hurts you
Take a personal object from him or her
Don't do anything against him or her
And it won't do anything to you.
If a spell you did wrong
There's something you must be sure
A very expensive price will be the cost
Multiply threefold that will be the payment
for you. Never be afraid and nothing will happen to
you everything you feel
You will keep under control
Everything is in your mind learn how to imagine
Everything you see and everything you feel.

Will never touch you. Anything is going to happen,
into the Protection Circle If you are in it, Everything

is going to be ok Fire, Air, Water and Earth with my
mind in silence. Anything is going to happen.
You won't ever know where I will be
Whether in front of the fire, Whether behind the
earth, Whether next to the air
Whether next to the water
And just because you won't ever know it
You will always be under my enchantment.

Everywhere and anywhere, wherever you will go, my
spell will go with you so.
If a love you want to catch, take a rose from a rose
bush, write the name and let it fly.

Without fear nor being scared
To the enchantment I'll walk in
With magical beings and fairies
At moon nights, The refuge I will find.

Between equals, witchcraft begins to work
Beware yourself of it, wear a necklace, a ring or a
thimble, let it on your place don't touch it anymore.

A needle and an egg, to the witch they belong,
With the magic of the mind, they give her the gift.

FINISHING THE RITUALS

Every magical operation is a different experience, the same way it starts in a quite state; it must be finished, with the same respect than starting it. Rituals have to be finished doing the inverse actions, which means, if you lighted the candles clockwise, you should put them off counterclockwise; this is a simple art, you also have to remember never putting off a candle by blowing it. In respect of the Circles of Protection, they are undone the same way, except for a ritual that requires another technique. Collect the used objects and materials, clean them well before putting them in their place. Keep the remaining wax of the candles to make a new one later; the rest of the materials like water or seeds have to be buried and never throw them out. At finishing, say a gratitude invocation to the Element you worked with.

*The Master **Kadaisha** said this, while looking at the immensity of the universe:*

"All you can see is yours, everything without limits. But there is a law you must have always present. Do not possess anything to avoid being possessed by anything".

CHAPTER IV

WITCHCRAFT PRACTICES

«The cost of wisdom is very high, that's why you can't buy it»

The following rituals are easy to practice and bring immediate answer in relation to monetary progress, increasing love, protection against energies of dark magic and increasing wellness; if you can't find some of the ingredients in your country, try to replace them with something similar, don't forget that witchcraft is the attraction of similar.

These operations must be done at the altar; isolation can generate conflict and misunderstanding within your nuclear family, that's why you need to have good relationships with people without the commitment to explain anything about your activities, the spirit of persecution hasn't stopped, even today, those who practice the occult sciences.

Keep following the steps previously explained in other chapters:

- Meditation and mental management
- Preparation of the altar
- Exorcisms
- Drawing the Circles of Protection
- Invocation
- Consummation of the ritual for sortileges
- Spells, filters and enchantments
- Termination of the rituals

If you need to do it at any place of your house, prepare a provisional altar and put it away later. This can be an awkward situation at the beginning, but in dribs and drabs you will discover another dimension of magic.

If you practice a ritual for another person, must earn some remuneration, witchcraft is not to be given as a present, or otherwise, the ritual won't work.

These practices will take effect rapidly and are samples for you to create yours.

CEREMONIES AND INITIATION IN WITCHCRAFT

You are going to enter in the world of magic, at this point we suppose that you already have read this book and are ready to practice the first ritual. Some of the most common practices are focused on finding harmony for the four wishes: protection of energies, health, prosperity and love; they are randomly ordered.

The Initiation is individual or collective:

Individual Initiation

It will work to be united with the four Elements and with this book; we are going to do it step by step as a sample for you to carry it on later:

Meditation: I'm a page of this book... you are hearing my voice in your mind... life and its changes are given to you here and now... rancor...hate... desires for revenge and fear will get away from your heart forever.

The value of the world is in your willpower... your discipline... your constancy...

You can do whatever you want... there's no limits... no more than those you impose.

You have the right to live plenty, under the sky and on the face of the earth... everything that exists is yours, take it... whatever is your concept about the first energy which is hidden in the small and the great, I give you the treasure of this book.

Fine! What are you wearing now? Do you feel comfortable in it? Do you think that would be better if you are naked to practice your first ritual in harmony with nature?

To practice this ritual, you will need:

• 2 white candles

- 2 black candles
- 1 feather of a bird (*white*)
- 1 feather of a bird (*black*)
- 1 pin
- Red and yellow flowers
- 1 yellow butterfly

Procedure: Draw a Circle of Protection with yellow and red petals, prepare the altar, put two white and two black candles on, they represent the balance among the Elements. They must be placed to the cardinal points first of all put a black candle to the North, a white one to the East, a black one to the South and a white one to the West; put this book in the middle of the star while lighting the candles.

At this moment, light the candle of the North and put some gold objects; let a yellow butterfly free.

Afterwards, light the other candles clockwise put on the altar the bowl with water and the little aquarium with the fish that will be free in a river.

Burn incense and spill aromas around the place, cinnamon is recommended; use the two feathers to move them over the book and the altar making circles, take the white feather with the left hand and the black feather with the right hand.

Put some stones and metals like: silver, bronze, magnetite, river stones on the space between the altar and the circle.

Keep the feathers crosswise over this page, making an X and pronounce aloud this exorcism:

*Eye, ye princeps principium, ens
entium, misere mei et respice in me servum
tuum N. Qui te devotissime invocate et te per
nomen tuum sactissimum tremendum.*

*Tetragramaton supplicat
Ut sis propicius et felix mihi in operationibus
Meis et jubeas angelis et spiritibus tuis
Venire et sedem in hoc loco ponere.*

*O vos omnes angeli spiritus stellarum,
o vos omnes angeli spiritus clementorum,
ó vos omnes spiritibus adstantes ante
faciem dei conjurat vos minister et servus fidelis
altissimi conjurat vos deus ipse ens entium o
tetragramaton, ut nunc et nunc veniatis et adsistatis*

huic operationi. Venite orat vos et supplicat
humilissime Servus dei.
Amén.

Offering the book to the North pronounce your name and say:

I invoke you, spirit of Fire.
For the power of the life, for the force of the love,
Oh, Seraph! Gladiator of the deep,
Between earth and heaven, you are.

You awake in my heart during rising
And chase away evil during setting.
Lead my mind at this time
To conjure this book to your grace
And presence. Put your shield of thunders to
Protect me from evil Be my protection to this
operation, that I now undertake with your
benevolence.

Offering to the East pronounce your name and say:

I invoke you, spirit of Air.
For the power of the life,
for the force of the love

Oh, Cherub! Gladiator of the deep,
Between earth and heaven, you are.

You awake in my mind during rising
And chase away evil during setting.
Lead my mind at this time
To conjure this book to your grace and presence.
Put your shield of hurricanes to
Get evil away be my protection to this
operation that I now undertake
with your benevolence.

Offering to the South pronounce your name and say:

I invoke you, spirit of Water.
For the power of the life,
for the force of the love
Oh, Tharsis! Gladiator of the deep,
Between earth and heaven, you are.
You awake in my blood during rising
And chase away evil during setting.
Lead my mind at this time
To conjure this book to your grace
And presence. Put your shield of ice to
Get evil cold be my protection to this operation
That I now undertake with your benevolence.

Offering to the West pronounce your name and say:

I invoke you, spirit of Earth.
For the power of the life, for the force of the love
Oh, Ariel! Gladiator of the deep,
Between earth and heaven, you are.
You awake in my mind during rising
And chase away evil during setting.
Lead my mind at this time
To conjure this book to your grace
And presence.
Put your shield of mountains to
Be my barrier against evil
Be my protection to this operation
That I now undertake with your benevolence.

At this point prick your middle finger of the left hand and put your fingerprint with a blood drop at the end of the following prayer:

I ask you angels and spirits
To give me wisdom to find the road.

I promise, swear and will accomplish
That I will never use this Grimoire
To hurt or damage

Nor obtaining benefit
At the expense of others,
On the contrary, I will use it
To soothe the pain of the souls.

En cados it moris
A tan ci mu loy
Que la az de et
Sea, sea, sea,
Ugi en der
Po en mi

Put your fingerprint here

Henceforth, practice meditation until the candles get consumed. Leave the book in the middle of the circle for three days without opening it, get out from it, opening it at any part and closing it, and do not pass over it. During the following days, extraordinary events will happen and you will perceive aromas (*like flowers and woods*), will have strange dreams, will find objects and will know people; it is the way of the angels to express their presence in your life. Nobody who has practiced this ritual has been without feeling the presences from nature.

There are not special hours or dates to do this conjuration with the book, if you are on the path of magic, will feel when the right moment is and when you are ready to do it.

Collective Initiation

This ritual is the representation of the Fire, Earth, Air and Water Elements to offer the book. It's practiced by four initiated, each one has to choose an Element to represent according to the personal vibration with the same. In case of being more than four people, organize groups of four in order to practice the ritual by separated groups; it's recommended to be in couples (*two men, two women*), if women are in their menstrual cycle, the ritual will be more powerful. Everyone needs to have its own book to be consecrated in this ceremony.

You will need:

- Virgin soil
- 7 red candles
- Wooden matches
- 7 incense cones
- 7 little crystal cups with water
- 7 black river stones
- 1 butterfly (*preferably a little and colored one*)
- 1 bird
- 1 fish
- 1 alive animal (*it can be a frog, a snail or a little snake*)
- 4 pins (*one per each participant*)

Procedure: Realize this ceremony naked or wearing a white large gown. It will be performed in an open field close to a river or the sea, at the third rising hour on Sunday under the influence of the New Moon.

We are responsible of clarifying that, during the practice of these magical rituals, there mustn't exist physical contact, only if you freely desire it. Unfortunately, a lot of women get raped by supposed wizards, who pretend having the knowledge of magical arts, taking advantage of the innocence; the search of benefits can result in damage, a real wizard doesn't try to have any physical contact because he knows the risks of energetic infestations.

Draw a Circle of Protection clockwise on the field with Virgin Soil; it must be wide enough for the four initiated to operate. Make a square in the middle of the circle as follows (*remember that as the lines are drawn, you have to continue in clockwise direction until closing the square*):

• **First Line:** The representative of the Fire Element draws the line of the square located to the North, using 7 red candles; light the first candle with wooden matches and use it to light the following candles, when finishing put the first candle on its place, go to the North and offering the butterfly say aloud:

Oh, angels of the night!
Salamanders of Fire and light
Purify this space,
And protect our skin
For the experience we undertake
At this moment.

I (*say your name*)
Invoke you, Spirit of Fire

Shelter of the North.
For the power of the life and love,
For the force of magic, I invoke you.
Oh, Seraph! Gladiator of the light,
Between heaven and earth, you are.
Lead our minds at this time
Be the shield of light in the darkness
Be our protection to this operation
That we now undertake.
To connect with your power
And your power comes to us.

At the end of the prayer let the butterfly free.

• **Second Line:** The representative of the Air Element draws the next line located to the East using 7 incense cones, burn one by one with wooden matches as placing them; at finishing, go to the East and offering the bird say aloud:

Oh, angels of the night!
Sylphs and Sylphids of Air
Purify this space,
And protect our magic and thoughts
For the experience we undertake
At this moment.

I (say your name)
Invoke you, Spirit of Air,
Shelter of the East.
For the power of the life and love,
For the force of magic, I invoke you.
Oh, Cherub! Gladiator of the winds,
Between heaven and earth, you are.
Lead our magic and thoughts at this time
Put your shield of hurricanes to transport the seed,
be our protection to this operation
That we now undertake.
To connect with your power
And your power comes to us.

At the end of the prayer let the bird free.

• **Third Line:** The representative of the Water Element draws the line located to the South using 7 little crystal cups with water; at finishing, go to the South and say aloud:

Oh, angels of the night!
Undines of Water, Purify this space,
And protect our blood
For the experience we undertake
At this moment.

I (say your name)
Invoke you, Spirit of Water,
Shelter of the South.
For the power of the life and love,
For the force of magic, I invoke you.
Oh, Tharsis! Gladiator of the seas,
Between heaven and earth, you are.
Lead our lives at this time
Be the shield of ice to cold evil
Be our protection to this operation
That we now undertake.
To connect with your power
And your power comes to us

After the ritual, the fish needs to come back to its habitat

• **Fourth Line:** The representative of the Earth Element draws the line located to the West using 7 black river stones; at finishing, go to the West and offering an alive animal say aloud:

Oh, angels of the night!
Magical beings and gnomes of the Earth
Purify this space and protect our body
For the experience we undertake
At this moment.

I (say your name)
Invoke you, Spirit of Earth,
Shelter of the West.
For the power of the life and love,
For the force of magic, I invoke you.
Oh, Ariel! Gladiator of the mountains,
Between heaven and earth, you are.

Lead our magic and thoughts at this time
Put your shield of valleys to be the path
Be our protection to this operation
That we now undertake.
To connect with your power
And your power comes to us.

The participants will sit within the circle, looking at the middle, keeping the corresponding cardinal point position according to the Element represented by each one. They will take their hands and rising their arms to heaven and then, putting them down on earth, each one will pronounce one word to symbolize its desire, to obtain the power of magic; for example: the participant of the North pronounces *"teaching"*, the next one pronounces *"helping"*, and so on. They must close the eyes for a few minutes; get ready, some physical effects will appear, wind, rain, strange sounds, etc.; keep calmed without breaking the union of hands without getting out from the circle.

Later, you all will give a name to the group, giving place to the baptism of the union you just have done; to seal the union, each one will prick his or her middle finger of the left hand and put the fingerprint on the others´ books right in the fields bellow without writhing your names.

Put your fingerprints here:

Fire

Water

Earth

Air

Practice meditation until the sunlight appears on the horizon; everything you see, feel, hear or perceive is only yours, do not make it public or speak about it; a good wizard or witch doesn't reveal his or her secrets, even when he or she is available to teach the magical arts, personal experiences are only his or hers.

About dawn, get away from the place of the ritual and leave your spirit in peace, getting out by your corresponding cardinal point this way: open a part of the circle carefully, take a step and then close the circle again; finally, walk away without looking back leaving the circle.

Get together to research, study and do group rituals. If one of the participants wants to quite, he or she can do it, it would be ideal not to do it but if he or she does, the book or Grimoire with the fingerprints has to be given to the group and the person can't be a part of the group again.

If the rest of the participants want to continue doing their collective work, they will complete the group with a new participant, making a new initiation ritual with new books and burning the old ones.

For Prosperity

Material abundance is not a synonym of spiritual evolution, it´s just a way to get it. Some people believe that poorness and conformism are virtues of masters.

Wisdom looks for living plenty, without getting opulence or presumption; you must have possessions as much as you need.

*The Master **Kadaisha** said:*

"The real wisdom shouldn´t be the act of accumulating only for others without obtaining a benefit from your work. Wisdom is in the mutual benefit for the possessor and those around him or her.
How can a hungry man talk to another about the bread´s flavor?"

• Realization of wishes:

Candles and water engender a ritual for the life, they unify in the first-quarter nights, allowing nature to gestate new ideas. This ritual is practiced in an open field.

You will need:

- 1 white candle
- A jar with water from the first quarter phase
- 1 moon's mirror (*no magnifying*)
- 21 river stones picked up during the Full Moon night
- Some fuel to do a circle of fire (*gas, alcohol, etc.*)

For the water, pick it up during a Full Moon or New Moon night in a ceramic bowl, put it on a fresh place in the open to receive the moon's influence, protecting it from the rays of the sun until you need to use it in a sortilege.

For the stones, pick up the 21 of them from a river or stream with your right hand during a Full Moon night, its better if they are small.

Procedure: during a Full Moon night, at the first setting hour, build the altar, invoke the angels and say the protection prayers, do a big circle with the 21 river stones and put the moon's mirror in the middle; make a canal in parallel to the circle to be filled with fuel (*be careful of causing a conflagration, use just the necessary to do a circle to be on fire for about fifteen minutes, use a little bit of fuel*), it's better if you do this on sand close to a river or the sea. Put the candle on the mirror, spill the water on the mirror until totally cover it.

Sit in front of the mirror (*in the lotus position*) and looking at the flame project your thought or wish to the future, imagine how you want to be within a time. Invoke the four Elements and throw the 21 stones in the canal clockwise, reaffirming with each stone, the meaning wish accompanied by your own spell. At throwing the last stone, put the canal on fire with the white candle, keep the mirror in the middle and wait for the fire to consume, meanwhile meditate about your wish.

At extinguishing the fire, take the stones carefully (*wait at least ten minutes before touching them*) clockwise and wash them with water from the jar. Keep them in a place where they don't get in contact with sunlight, and the second night of the first-quarter phase, throw them backwards to a river. Don't forget to cover the canal of the fire.

Important: Do not keep any stone as an amulet, this action will annul the effect of the other stones, in addition, the candle must totally consume.

In case of practicing this ritual for harvesting abundance, you must use seeds of the plants to sow; afterwards, the seeds have to be placed at each corner of the farm.

• Wine Conjuration

Candles and angels please certain wishes; our life is full of chances and possibilities of changing; the following ritual is useful to get the power to create alternatives for your life:

You will need:

- 7 different yellow flowers
- 7 candles with the colors of the rainbow
- 1 moon's mirror
- 7 different grains (*rice, beans, etc.*)

• 1 bottle of wine

Procedure: During the course of the first-quarter phase, on Friday at setting, light the candles on a large circle clockwise around the altar and the other circles; then put the mirror in the middle with the seeds and the wine on it; put a flower in front of each candle in the inside. Invoke the four Elements, take the grains which represent the seed of abundance, and put them in the wine or champagne.

With your eyes closed and concentrating, keep your image in mind, seeing yourself this way: imagine a mountain and you are sitting on the top, wearing white, see yourself serene and happy. Frame the vision in an orange sun in the background (*in other words, see a sunrise while sitting on the top of the mountain*), the sun raises and doesn't decline, you will be alone; after doing that, pull off the petals of the flowers and drop them in the wine or champagne, pick them up counterclockwise, bury the wax in some place.

At dawn, on Saturday, at the moon hour, take a shower with the wine or champagne; spray your house or business with this bath. Don't forget to recite the invocations to the spirits of nature, and now get ready to receive the changes that will come unexpectedly.

Bury the petals and seeds in a flowerpot indoors and wait for them to germinate, if they do, transplant them individually in other flowerpots. These plants are magnetized and will be magic for good.

• Sortilege of the Broom

In order to find abundance and prosperity for the house, we work the symbolism of food and money.

You will need:

- 1 new broom
- 1 needle
- 2 pieces of thread (*black and white*)
- 1 bill (*denomination doesn't matter*)
- 7 different grains
- 1 four-life clover

Procedure: on Saturday or Sunday, in the morning, put in the broom bristles the seven grains and the bill (*you can stick them to still there while sweeping*). Immediately sweep the house from outside to inside.

In the course of the day, with the needle threaded (*with the two pieces*), sew up a point in the right pocket of the head of the household's pants (*no matters if it's only one or two people*). much better if it is possible to do the operation with all the pants. It's recommended making a little imperceptible stitch.

At night, put the 7 grains, the bill and the clover in a place to receive the moon's influence (*window, yard, terrace, etc.*) in order to attract magical beings of abundance. Don't worry if something misplaces that's a sign of the presence of magical beings. Next day, put them all with your personal objects.

• Money Sortilege

This sortilege can be done in any last-quarter night at 9 p.m. using a personal object and a representation of money to keep it with you.

You will need:

- 1 green kerchief
- 3 leaves of purple or white basil
- 1 bill (*denomination doesn't matter*)
- 1 label taken from a personal piece of clothing

- Amber oil
- 1 four-colored candle (*representing the four elements*)
- Abundance seeds

Procedure: On the altar, light the four-colored candle and put on the kerchief the three basil leaves, the bill, the label and the abundance seeds; get the seed from the amber oil out and put it on too. Spill wax of the candle on the objects, do the same with some drops of oil. Afterwards, tie up the kerchief making a knot with the four ends. Let the candle consuming all night long.

• New Moon's Spell

At this new moon time, the powers of the Fire get stronger to benefit people, It's time to gestate ideas and projects for their realization.

You will need:

- 1 gold-pointed needle
- Yellow thread
- River stones

This sortilege brings the force to start new projects, the initiation, either for your business, work, projects or relationships.

Procedure: in a New Moon night, at an odd hour, sew the river stone with the yellow thread to the left side of one of your sweaters; put other two river stones under your bed and another in your room's doorframe, they have to stay there for seven days with their nights. Afterwards, take them away and put them in the open (*in a park, field, etc.*) to allow them come back to nature. The force of the stones together with the New Moon fire will embody your wishes and projects in reality.

• **Work Sortilege**

As well as personal energy harmonizes with nature, your wishes and projects will establish until finding realization.

You will need:

- Stone oil
- Magnetite (*stone of natural magnet*)
- Four-colored candle

- 1 Small black fabric bag
- 14 basil leaves (*preferably purple basil*)

Procedure: In a Tuesday or Friday night, put out in the open a bowl with the oil, the magnetite and the leaves in it. Light the candle for one hour, and so on during the following nights until the candle gets totally consumed. In the morning, after taking a shower, put the oil on your body, remember putting the stones in the bag after using the oil, and later put the bag underneath your pillow in order to irradiate your energy while sleeping.

From now on, put one of the basil leaves in your left pocket and another in your right shoe, day and night. The following days you will replace the used leaves with new ones during seven days.

Likewise, whenever you have an interview or a meeting, carry the magnetite with you to increase your energy, it is recommended to put two purple basil leaves the day before, in the pair of shoes you will wear.

• Prosperity Enchantment

The symbolism of Fire has been associated with humanity like the power and force to concrete ideas and projects.

You will need:

- 1 White candle
- 1 Energy Channeler

This ritual is practiced on a Wednesday or Friday to attract the energetic power from the moon to channel it to you.

That night (*of the day you prefer*), at an odd hour (*7, 9, 11 p.m.*), light the candle for one hour, during that time you need to be calm and have loving and kindness thoughts to enforce the moon's influence for your wishes to come true.

Going by one hour, put the candle off and keep it. Do the same operation for seven consecutive nights (*the seventh night, if there's some wax left, bury it*).

Next morning after the first night of the ritual, put some oil drops on your house's corners for seven mornings, preferably at the same hour until consuming the entire oil.

• Spell of Power

The secret lies in the contact with the forces of nature and let them flow softly, to unite their powers with you and your operations.

You will need:

- Water from the last-quarter phase
- 1 yellow candle
- 1 white stone
- Artemisia leaves

Procedure: On Monday or Wednesday, at night, at an odd hour (*7, 9 or 11 p.m.*), light the yellow candle on the white stone, this is done on the altar; while the candle consumes be calm and in a meditative attitude. The main objective is to cover the stone with wax from the candle to have it with you in your wallet, purse or underneath the pillow, in order to conserve this energy.

Next morning, while taking a shower, rinse your body with the water from the last-quarter. To enforce your wish of power, try to have an Artemisia plant with you (*at home, or at work*) or at least, some leaves or twigs.

• Invoking Magical Beings

These beings have been over time, those "*in charge*" of turning into reality the material wishes of humanity, obtaining in return gifts and presents they love.

You will need:

• 2 blue candles
• 1 cigarette
• The left shoe (*previously polished*) of those who are a part of this work (*This could be done to obtain something or to progress*)
• 1 broom (*the one you use at home*)

Procedure: At the first night of the last-quarter phase, at an even hour (*8, 10, and 12*) put the two candles and the cigarette shaping a triangle with them (*the cigarette on top*), light the candles on the altar. Recite the prayer of the Spirits of Nature, being totally calm and in a meditative attitude. Let the candles totally consume.

At the same time, place the polished left shoe(s) and the broom close to the front door, and pulverize the cigarette around them; Leave those objects there until next morning.

The remaining wax and cigarette rests must be swept with the same broom, from the outside to the inside; pick up and put them in a place where they can go with the wind.

To avoid the lack of food

Attracting the influence of nature using symbols has been a tradition since the Celtic Culture times.

Get a whole wheat bread and cut it into 13 slices which you are going to share out among partners or members of your family. Take a crumb from each slice before giving it and keep them all.

You will need:

- 13 rice grains
- 13 beans
- 13 coins of the same value

Procedure: This ritual is practiced on Friday in the first-quarter phase at 9 p.m., get the ingredients together to put them in a small fabric bag which has to be put on the backside of the front door or your room's door.

Leave the bag there until next Friday of the first-quarter phase when you will pick it up to leave it outside in the open.

This ritual can be carried out every month to attract abundance and prosperity for you.

• The Power of Nature

The recipes to work using seeds represent the beginning, the fecundation.

You will need:

- 1 mango seed
- 7 green candles
- 1 pin or needle

Procedure: Put the mango seed under sunlight for seven days, then, clean it well until getting a residue-free surface.

At the first night of the last-quarter phase write backwards (*from right to left*) on the seed with the pin or needle your wish and name.

At an odd hour of the same night, put the candles shaping a circle clockwise on the altar surrounding the seed, light them equally clockwise and say the following prayer:

«Oh, Spirits of the light who
live in heavenly spaces
I (*say your name*)
Invoke you at this solemn hour to come
To this little altar of Fire
That I´ve founded in your honor,
Jeliel, Sitael, Gaziel, Ariel, Michael, Raphael and
Gabriel Spill your virtues over this Place
Open up your gold-bearing wings
And cover my house with them
To live happy and be absolutely healthy,
And see myself realized with
Every kind of prosperities.

And, as a proof of my love for you all
Spirits of heavenly light
In which I have made the mysterious signs
To please you, for happiness to reign
In my house for the seven days of the week».

Let the candles alight for half an hour, put them off and the following six nights light them one by one.

Keep the seed in a safe place during those days while consuming the candles, the last night take the seed and bury it (*in a flowerpot or field*) to germinate your wishes.

• For Abundance

This ritual is made on Thursday or Saturday of the last-quarter phase.

You will need:

- Soil
- 2 yellow candles
- 3 seeds of a red fruit
- A piece of white fabric
- 1 bill or coin
- 1 cigarette

- 1 glass of wine

Procedure: The chosen night, make a rag doll that you'll name "*Feing*" (*write the name on the doll with a thread or marker*), Next morning you will get it together with the rest of the ingredients.

The next day, while daylight is coming, get backwards in your bedroom dispersing the soil, light the candles on each side of the place and put the rag doll in the middle, spill the wine and put the cigarette on its body.

Afterwards, write on a paper the petition you wish (*food, clothing, lands, money, etc.*), bury the doll with the seeds, the remaining wax of the candles, the soil and the letter in a flowerpot, park or field.

• Footwear Spell

You will need:

- An old pair of your shoes
- A bunch of seven different plants (*one of those must be basil*) tied with a green ribbon
- 1 four-colored candle
- 1 magnetite (*natural magnet*)

- 1 energy channelizer
- 1 black small fabric bag

Procedure: At the altar, take the bunch and shake it around the shoes to clean energy. Do the same operation at your front door or your bedroom's door (*inside*). Upon finishing, place the shoes as if they were taking a step in from the door (*the right shoe goes forward*), put the candle in the middle of them (*this represents the walker's light*), light it and put the magnetite in the right shoe. Meditate during nine minutes about everything you want for your life, it is important that the candle gets totally consumed.

The following dawn, polish the shoes and the door inside with a piece of fabric previously impregnated with the energy channeler and put the magnetite in a black small fabric bag. Take the bunch out of you house the same morning. Carry with you the bag with the magnetite inside for 23 days and don't say anything about this practice.

• The Fire of Prosperity

An antique magic recipe consists in practicing the fire ritual while getting on for dawn, when the first rays of the sun appear on the horizon.

You will need:

- 7 yellow candles
- 1 spark of gold
- Abundance seeds
- Wheat grains
- Green grape seeds
- Black grape seeds
- Black soil
- Water from the New Moon
- Virgin soil: you can get this soil by digging 20 centimeters approximately to be sure that nobody has walked on it, it would be better if it's mud or clay.
- Cinnamon sticks

Procedure: light seven yellow candles within the three circles of protection. In the middle of the circles put in a bowl the spark of gold, an abundance seed, one wheat grain, two green grape seeds, one black grape seed and virgin soil.

Invoke the Fire Elementals and mix the ingredients with water from the New Moon, shake it seven times to the right and then strain it to remove the water, making a homogeneous mud paste with the seeds in it; mold a sphere and let it dry under sun.

When the sphere gets dry, keep it in a green bag and carry it with you for seven days, at the end of which you will put the sphere in a nest made with cinnamon sticks placed over the front door frame.

Abundance will appear unexpectedly, in case of getting lost or melted the sphere because of the water; the effect of the ritual will disappear, same if someone takes off the sphere, that person will take your positive energy.

• Conjuration of the Broom

You will need:

- 7 different grains
- 7 yellow flowers
- 2 brown candles
- 1 Energy Channelizer
- Broom

Procedure: On Tuesday or Friday night put the petals and the grains at the four corners of your house. The next day, at dawn take the broom and sweep the grains and petals. At finishing, light the two candles in the front door (*if don't, do it in your bedroom*) and pronounce the following conjuration:

Taer iŋ eŋ et es zada
Pique cia y el de la posŋame
Fusi aq se daŋ odui
Clo de porauŋ el ab lader.

Spill some drops of the channeler (*while the candles are lit*) shaping a circle to the left of the door and a triangle to the right. Pick up the objects and the rests and get them out of your house. Leave the candles lit for one hour and then put them off, the remaining ones must be lit during the following seven days until consuming.

• Sugar on the last-quarter phase

During this phase of the moon the earth's influences harmonize with its Elements, that fact helps human being to concrete wishes focused on personal benefit. You will only use some sugar and garlic. On Friday or Saturday, at 7 p.m., melt the sugar and cover the garlic with it on the altar. When the garlic gets cold, divide it into four pieces and put them in four different places of your house (*or your bedroom*).

Note: It is important to divide the garlic in a place where it is possible to be under the moon's influence (*yard, window, etc.*) after dividing the garlic, put it out all night long to receive the influence.

Leave the pieces of garlic for three days in their places, the fourth day you will bury them (*in a flowerpot, yard or garden*) to materialize your petition and getting them back to nature. It is recommended to make an economic (*salary, pay increases, work, business, money, etc.*).

• **The Power of the Moon**

The Water Element produces great benefits to obtain abundance; there are some formulas which cause almost immediate effects. Remember that money is not happiness, even being a way to find it.

You will need:

- 1 coin or gold medal
- Champagne

Procedure: Perform this ritual on the first day of the first-quarter phase, take the coin or medal and immerse it in a recipient with water, invoke the Water Element, then, keep it in a place away from the sunlight until the first Full Moon night. At midnight, close to a well, after making the preceding ritual, throw the coin or medal in the well, asking for your wish, while doing it you must order but never beg, it works better if you decree. It is important that the moon gets reflected on the water of the well at the moment of throwing the coin or medal. This enchantment also can be practiced close to a river or the sea in December.

Getting a successful job

Light 4 green candles on Tuesday, put some seeds of fruits of the same color (*apple, pear, etc.*) next to the candles, and invoke the Earth Elementals. Keep the seed protected from the sunlight, the following morning mix the seed in a litter of water and take a bath with it.

With the remaining wax of the candles, polish your shoes (*the ones you will use for appointments and interviews*); magical beings feel a special attraction for shoes. The seed has to be buried in a place close to your house.

At dawn on Sunday, find 7 rice grains and put them on a moon's mirror. Light a red candle in the middle of the mirror invoking the Fire Element, at the same time recite the following words:

> For the power of the light
> For the power of the Fire and the Air
> That the land abounds for my service.
>
> That this rice grows to the infinite.
> Cados aet mi en
> Et su Ter.

Let the candle totally consume and keep the mirror in its place avoiding contact with sunlight. Before Sunday, give the rice grains to your neighbors or co-workers. It is better if you practice this ritual during the last-quarter phase.

Quick formulas

• **How to get progress in business:** There are some methods to keep balance and constant advance and progress without being ambitious; magic always works if you don't cross the line between being and having.

If your desire is advancing, light nine brown candles in your place of work during the last-quarter phase on Sunday and spread mustard seeds around the place. Invoke the Elements; at night, let an old shoe and a four-leaf clover in the open to receive the zephyrs´ influence, they will attract gnomes, genie from the earth.

In as much as you advance, open up your life to kindness, and be balanced without falling in greed. **For example:** sometimes donate something to a person in need, don't allow the beneficiary to know the origin of the donation.

• **To increase sales and customers**: On a Thursday night, put seven white feathers and one black, and a black candle at a window facing the street; light the candle using a cinnamon stick or some aromatic piece or wood, let the wind or zephyr to transport the feathers, before doing this invoke the angels of Air and Earth.

Put the feathers on the palm of the left hand and blow them to the sky invoking your wish, after that put the candle off. During the next seven days light the candle for a while before opening the doors of your business. This ritual will be more powerful and will have greater influence if you put one coin or bill under the candle, and the next day put it in the place to keep money (cash register) being careful of never giving it to anyone. At passing the seven days and having the seven coins or bills, stand up backwards to the business´ door and throw them to the street without looking back.

• **To increase your incomes:** Smoke up a coin with a yellow candle, the coin must be obtained from a bank; on Sunday, Wednesday and Friday at the sun hours (*noon*) put the coin on a place where is publicly visible. During those days is important to light a red candle (*remember invoking the Water Elementals: Undines, Nodites and Nereides*).

• **To attract progress:** Find a red or white altar candle which has been previously lighted in a sanctuary or temple; when taking it, put it off with your left hand and invoke the salamanders. Divide the altar candle into seven cuts without breaking it and put a coin into each one of the cuts, light it and as the candle goes consuming, the coins release one by one, put the coins on the top of the front door, at obtaining the last one put it in a little green fabric bag which must be hanging behind the door. Light a white candle and spill seven wax drops over the bag every change of moon.

To obtain the promotion you are waiting for: If you think you have the skills to be promoted, put on the altar three yellow candles on Tuesday, write on them the angels' symbols (*See the symbols of the four Elements' Princes in the Grimoire*) who govern the four cardinal points, as well as the name of the person who wants to be promoted (*write the name bottom-up*), place the candles forming a triangle, and put a picture where the person looks excellently dressed in the middle of them. Pronounce the spell that you wish; remember that it should be said as a rhyme and imperatively aloud.

In some cases, the force of the invoked energy is so strong that it could bring better alternatives for you, they would emerge after difficult moments. For example: you can lose your current job, but will get a better one; if this happens, do not reject, on the contrary think that better events are coming; at getting unsettled you will neutralize the effect of your wish.

Energies are kind, they don't work according to the human being's whims; for them, if you lose a job, it doesn't mean anything because they know that you will find something better.

• **The Fire Spark:** During the Full Moon phase, light three white candles on the altar and take one bill or coin, pick some wax from the candles and mix it with the money, put it together with a personal object which contains your energy, it's better if you use a picture; this ritual is to harmonize your energies with money using Fire. Any time you need money, keep *"The Fire Spark"* with you and leave a little bit of wax in the place where you want to see your purpose accomplished.

Materialize your wishes: Being inside the Circles of Protection, light four candles: red, green, blue and white; forming a square with them, surround each candle with Fire Sand and put a bowl with water (*if possible from a river*) into the square. Use the Thurible to burn some sandal, myrrh and petals of three yellow flowers. Sit down facing the south, focus on your wish, create a mental image as clear as possible, and feel it as real. See yourself already possessing what you desire, after a few minutes open your eyes and stop thinking about your vision.

Store the objects you used very respectfully. Ambition and anxiety may annul your ritual; a few days later, if your wish comes to help your personal and spiritual development, it will be given to you through an unexpected way.

Other formulas

In order to maintain the flow of positive energies at home or in your company, use cinnamon as an air freshener, stick a little bit of it behind the doors. Initiate this ritual on Sunday at 7 p.m. and renew it every 7 days.

Every Full Moon Tuesday before sunrise, clean your house using seven bitter herbs cook in water without boiling them. Take two lemons and break them in cross, seven yellow carnations a four-leaf clover, recite the Earth Element Invocation, incense the entire house and proceed to clean it up.

• Formulas for Home

For the living room: It belongs to the Air Element, projects communication, exerts influence on business and home energies.

Ritual: Do it on Wednesday at rising, invoking the Air Elementals. Light a yellow candle while you are thinking of your wish.

For the bedroom: It belongs to the Earth Element; it works in gestating new ideas, projects and plans, trips, new jobs, societies and improving health. The ritual is done at the third setting hour, on Friday and under the influence of Venus.

Ritual: Light a green candle in front of a mirror joined with two yellow feathers and a golden butterfly. If the butterfly dies it is a presage of accidents and calamity, neutralize it giving a purple set of sheets to someone who needs it.

Dining room: It belongs to the Earth Element; it projects wishes of abundance, represents society and family communion. It's also connected with concepts of mental and intellectual development, nourishment is not only physical but spiritual too. Be careful with this place because according to the tradition, it is right there where death happens (*of somebody or of some situation*).

Ritual: Use a black candle and a whole wheat bread sprinkled with salt. Do it at the last setting hour on Monday, at sunrise; crumble the bread and put it at a window or terrace to be eaten by birds. Invoke the Earth Elementals, magical beings and gnomes.

Kitchen: Fire Element. Symbolizes purification; for example, if you feel that every event of your life goes wrong or a distressing time has come, it is the moment for fire to purify changes, protect against love treats and enforce feelings.

Ritual: Do it at the setting hours, use three candles (*red, white and blue*), light them until getting totally consumed, and invoke the angels of the Elements. It is prudent to wash the kitchen with fire sand and once in a while use a double purple candle to maintain the sentimental union. In case of seeing food spoilage at home or milk gets sour; those are signs of negative energies irradiation and possibly failure will come if you don't make decisions on time.

Front door: Air Element. It works to avoid energetic infestation in case of having unpleasant visits.

Ritual: Put a broom upside down (*with the brush upside*) and light a blue candle to neutralize evil effluvium, do it on Friday at setting. Invoke the Fire Elementals. Put the candle off with water from the New Moon. If unexpected events come to your life, light a yellow candle on Tuesday at rising.

Courtyard: this place combines the four Elements.

Ritual: Do it at midnight in a Full Moon night with 2 brown candles. Take some amber oil, 7 bitter plants and one lemon; prepare a bath with the plants and the oil, break the lemon in cross and put it in the middle of the courtyard. Spread the courtyard with the preparation and sweep it to the middle. Pick up the rests, put them in a green bag and bury. Abundance and prosperity will be present.

Bathroom: Water Element. It is also known as the place of changes, it is the place for organic and emotional evacuation that must be constantly energetically clean.

Ritual: Open all the taps fully for a few seconds while lighting 5 white candles and invoke the Water Elementals: Undines, Nodites and Nereides; at the third sun hour during the last-quarter phase, Burn a piece of cedarwood and close the bathroom for three hours. Do this whenever you feel negative influences reflected on your personal and sentimental deals. Put four drops of wax of the candle at each corner of the mirror, and please don't cry in the bathroom because you can contaminate other people who use it.

Work place: Earth Element. Light everyday candles of different colors, join them with flowers of the same color of the candle you light. Take the petals off the flowers while the candle is consuming; if the flowers wither too fast, it is a sign of psychic energies infestation and you will need to exorcise the place because someone is damaging you.

For Love

Practice these rituals in the nights of waning and Full Moon; if the enchantment is to influence another person, concentrate and imagine that person the way you want to see him or her. Remember that feelings don't have to be imposed, if someone doesn't love you do not insist, these rituals are to increase thinking but not to change mental concepts; they will give you a different energy and a great power of attraction over the opposite gender.

At the beginning, light seven candles invoking the Air Element (*see the Grimoire*), write backwards on a paper the name of the person you want to attract, focus on your wish, look at the flames, allows the candle to consume totally. During the seven days of the waning moon phase, light a red candle at rising.

• The Orange Tree

An ancient formula of Magick to get couples spiritually together is performed with the orange in a flower, as a way to conjure energy.

Procedure: During a Full Moon night, when the flower falls and the fruit is born, take two oranges and halve them, half for man, half for woman and leave on the tree the two other halves. Afterwards, hugging together, give the juice from your half to each other; being interwoven for the power of the Fire, Earth, Air and Water.

When finishing, you will interchange the seeds which will keep with you forever as a promise of love. When blooming and if the tree gives fruits, abundance and happiness will come for those who practice this ancient magical art, increasing their wishes.

This ritual has a condition: those who practice this ritual and then want to separate the united (*which can never happen*) or betray the promise of love by cheating on the other or destroying your couple, will be punished by the Elements which will be against you forever.

Magic is not a game, before practicing rituals, please ensure about being in love with your couple. Enchantments made cannot be unmade and conjurations will accomplish three times.

• Sandal Enchantment

This may be the ritual that requires the influence of the Air Element the most. Love rituals and their magical formulas go from thought to thought, unifying two beings.

You will need:

- Underwear of your couple
- 2 red candles
- 3 roses
- Fire sand
- Sandal aroma
- 1 wine or champagne bottle

Procedure: In the Full Moon nights take the underwear with the personal energy of you both, they must be used and unwashed; interweave them in the middle of the circles of protection. Put the red candles and roses on the altar, draw two interweaved rings with fire sand, burn some sandal aromas in the Thurible and put the wine or champagne bottle in a bowl, as a symbol of union.

Light the candles and put the petals off the flowers, place them into the fire sand rings with the rest of the objects. If possible, use two pictures; get your hands close to the objects at reading the Air Element invocation to unify energies. At finishing, rub yourself with the wine or champagne firmly thinking about your beloved, tie the underwear making nine knots and pronouncing the following enchantment:

«Everything tied
on Earth, will be
tied in heaven»

This ritual can't be done for those who have betrayed or physically hurt their beloved ones, use it only when relationships are having difficulties caused by envy and jealousy. Lovers are eternal and hide in the Full Moon nights. Men and women who have sponsored abortion don't try this, the cosmos forces will be always against you.

*The Master **Kadaisha** said:*

**«The decease of an innocent is paid day after day,
And silent nature does not forgive,
Nobody who destroys a life can be in peace».**

• **Love Spell**

You will need:

• 4 candles (*green, red, blue and yellow*)
• 4 bowls with moon water
• Sandal essence

Procedure: This spell is practiced with four bowls with moon water shaping a square representing the four cardinal points, and with four candles (*green, red, blue and yellow*).

Drop the sandal essence in the four bowls, the couple will be into the circles of protection and shouldn't have had sexual relations at least five days before this enchantment. It is better if they are naked and nearby a creek spring. Invoke the Four Elements at being into the magical circles (*see the Grimoire*).

After practicing the ritual, rub each other with water from the bowls into the circles of protection, each one will put off two candles. Some couples have sexual relations before unmaking the circles; this act will get them united forever.

Taking personal objects from a couple and conjuring them in a Full Moon night get the couple mentally together instead of being physically separated; thanks to the same objects, each one of them will know what the other is living and feeling. Loyalty is mandatory for those who practice this ritual.

• To get them together

Personal objects taken from the two members of the couple are used to enforce love and union.

You will need:

• 3 green apple seeds
• 1 needle with black and white thread

- 1 red kerchief
- 3 red rose petals
- The label from your couple and your underwear
- 1 ounce of Love Perfume
- 1 red candle

Procedure: It's done in the first night of last-quarter phase at rising, light the candle to get consumed in the middle of the altar. Take the two labels and put them together (*like making a bag*), sew them with the two threads letting a small hole to put the apple seeds inside, which will receive the spell of your wish; remember pronouncing it as a rhyme and aloud:

«*I conjure you*
With these seeds
To become our love into eternal...»

Wrap everything with the red kerchief including the petals and set it next to the candle for about fifteen minutes, and then put the candle off.

The next morning, in the bathroom, put some love perfume on your body. It is recommended to wear that day the socks inside out and also trim the ends.

Bury the kerchief with the objects in a garden full of flowers or next to a leafy and resistant tree (*it can be indoors or outdoors*). Consume the remaining candle the same night.

From now on and for nine days, be in an indifferent mode with your couple. This will enforce the feelings of that person for you.

• For Spelling

It is performed looking at mirrors.

You will need:

- 1 little round mirror
- 1 red candle
- Water from the last-quarter phase

Procedure: This experience should be preferably practiced during the phase of New or Full Moon. At any night, in a dark room, sit in front of a mirror and put the candle on the altar to your right avoiding the candle to be reflected in the mirror.

Light the candle for 20 minutes and then put it off, focus your gaze in the middle of the mirror imagining the person you yearn for, commanding what you want to happen (*a call, a visit, etc.*) and saying the spell as a rhyme:

«Come on, come on
Nothing stops you to return»

Note: While imagining, try to think only of the person you are interested in; if you think of another person, there is a high risk of sending the irradiation of the ritual to that third person.

The following days procure that the person you are interested in, sees itself reflexed in the mirror (*with any pretext*). At night, light the candle, smoke the mirror and write the name of the person backwards.

Next morning, after taking your shower, put some water from the last-quarter on your skin to harmonize your energy with the environment. Keep or bury the mirror.

• Willow's Spell

This tree increases the power of love and relationships. Realize this ceremony in a Full Moon night. The power of the Air raises feelings.

Get a willow bark and at an odd hour of the same night, write on it vertically your name and horizontally the name of the person you are interested in, being those cross-shaped. Recite the following prayer holding the willow bark with your right hand:

To raino se ama
Lo que jamás se separa
Qui se at, quise re
Con esto ya lo ten che.

Bur the willow bark with the fire of a candle, let the ashes blow away with the wind towards the beloved person. The candle will be lit for one hour. From next night on, light it until getting totally consumed.

• Elderflowers in Full Moon

In the first full moon night, get three elderflowers, a moon's mirror and a brown candle. At nine p.m. of the same day put the mirror on the altar and the elderflowers on it shaping a triangle, light the brown candle in the middle of the flowers for fifteen minutes, thinking of three wishes at the same time. Put the candle off and keep it in a place away from sunlight. Next night do the same operation until the candle is totally consumed. Put an elderflower in the right pocket of a piece of clothing you wore the same day (*sweater, pants, etc.*); put another one in the left pocket and the third flower on your bedroom's door.

The next morning take the flowers and put them underneath your mattress until the next Full Moon when you have to take them out and throw them into a river.

• Venus´Love

You will need:

- Underwear
- 3 threads (*red, green, white*)
- 1 needle
- Venus Perfume
- 3 roses
- 1 black and 1 white buttons

Procedure: Sew with the three threads the buttons on the underwear of the person you want to enchant (*one over the other*). Make it preferably on Friday or Tuesday and that night go to bed with the piece of underclothing.

Put the petals of the red flowers and the piece of underclothing under your sheet to the middle for three days and nights. At the third day, mix the perfume, petals and underwear in a litter of water. Remove the buttons, and dispose of the water, petals and threads. During the same day, leave the buttons in a garden or park full of flowers.

Whenever you want to attract your couple or simply irradiate an intense energy use that underwear. Be especially careful with your personal appearance and keeping an indifferent attitude with the opposite gender or your couple.

• Blackberry Ritual

You will need:

- Blackberry seeds
- 1 black candle
- 1 white candle

- Some elder leaves
- 1 moon's mirror
- 3 red candles
- 1 blood drop from your middle finger
- 2 white feathers (*preferably of a dove*)
- 3 blue candles previously magnetized in the full moon
- 16 red rose petals
- Fire sand

Procedure: In the first-quarter night, take half a litter of water from a river in a glass container; preserve it in a place away from sunlight until next Full Moon.

In the full moon night, use the water to prepare an essence; put in it the blackberry seeds, 16 rose petals, elder leaves and a little bit of fire sand, put the preparation under moon influence. During the same night put the six candles around the mirror (*which is lying down with the reflecting side facing up*) shaping a circle counterclockwise and alternating red with blue.

Equally important, light blue and red candles counterclockwise around the circle and finally light the white and the black ones which symbolize the couple in the middle of the mirror. Prick your middle finger of the left hand with a sterilized pin or needle and put a blood drop on the mirror between the two candles and put the feathers on the sides of the blood drop. Write backward the name of your beloved person with the needle using your blood as ink and invoke at that moment the Air Elementals.

Stay a half an hour in the place listening to soft music to concentrate and meditate. Take the essence you prepared (*previously filtered*) and put it on your body. Put the candles off and leave all the objects you used to perform this ritual in front of the mirror until dawn. Afterwards, go to a high open place (*mountain, building, terrace or window*) and blow the feathers to the wind pronouncing the following magical words:

(Say the name of the person
you are interested in)
Te qui te paero...
Igo co atraam)...
No es ato momera...
Uno que mo...
Uno que co tenin)...

During the following days (*while still being in the same moon phase*), light a daily candle alternating red and blue. After this ceremony, it is very important to change your look (*hair, dressing, etc.*), when meeting the desired person be left indifferent and when you look at his or her eyes keep in mind the conjuring and the image of the feather.

Quick formulas

How to attract the person you are interested in: At setting on Friday, light with your left hand two red candles to the north and to the south, invoke the Air Elementals. Write backwards on a piece of parchment the name of the person and your wish. Take two seeds of a red fruit (*apple, plum, grape, etc.*) and a white feather with your right hand; cover the seeds with wax of the candles while saying the name of the desired person.

Burn the parchment with the name written on, and on Sunday at the first sunlight hour, throw the feather to the wind pointing to the desired person's place.

Leave the seeds previously covered with wax in a church and at the same time imagine a wedding. This ritual gets more powerful if is done in a Full Moon night, after doing it you should wear red.

• **Love Awakening:** During the last-quarter night at the second setting hour, light three candles: red, white and yellow; write on the three of them the names of the couple, the woman's name horizontally and the man's name vertically cross-shaped, and pronounce the following magical words:

Do camis en el dengid
At ata ata at fecer a mi.

Wear yellow underclothing that night. Don't forget to invoke the Air Elementals. With the remaining wax of the candles make a heart that contains some personal object from the person you are interested in.

To chase away those people who interfere with your relationship: Get a new white kerchief and three hairs of a black cat. In a New Moon night at the first rising hour, write on the kerchief the name of who interferes with your relationship, light a black candle and smoke the name, take the kerchief's ends and make seven knots, baste the ends with a needle using the braided cat hairs as thread; throw the kerchief to a river or stream. Let the candle on until consuming and keep pronouncing the spell.

The intruder will be chased away from your life, remember that love has to be cultivated with fine details. Before practicing this ritual think about your acts, if they are to hold on loving or at the contrary you have put aside your couple. Remember to invoke the Air Elementals.

• **Couple's Harmony:** Green and blue candles work to change mood. In a waning moon night, take some cinnamon sticks and put them behind your bedroom's door, at the same time light two candles (*green and blue), draw a triangle under your bed with melted wax (still watery)*. Seven days later, take the triangle and the cinnamon out and bury them. Light blue and green candles during the following seven days, alternating the colors every night (*Remember to invoke the Air Elementals*).

Increase your power of seduction with the opposite gender (*Attraction and magnetism*): In the Full Moon night use three candles, one mirror and one small bowl with water. Light the candles next to the mirror to reflex their image; the melted wax has to fall into the water. Take the bowl with your right hand and pass it under your belly making three circles this way: one to the right, one to the left and the last one over the navel (*half circle to the left and half circle to the right*). After practicing this ritual, change your look (*dressing, hair, etc.*) and prepare the following enchanting perfume:

- 13 honey drops
- 2 white roses
- 1 red rose
- Cinnamon or anise water
- 1 white feather
- Mineral oil

On Sunday at rising, mix the ingredients (*excepting the feather*) in a pot and put it on the heat until boiling, stir the preparation with the feather and pronounce the following magical words:

Ed ed ed por cados

Ef gasar in tu mallal

I (say your name)

Et et et on mi ter

Que alger que damer

Se tra se tra un ser.

After this conjuring, recite the Air Element invocation.

This perfume is to be used on the lower abdomen every night until the next Full Moon phase.

• **Marriage:** In the first New Moon night, light seven white candles, burn two white feathers and pick up the ashes. Make two interlaced circles with fire sand; write in them with your finger the names of the couple. Put the candles in the middle of the circles and spread the ashes over the feathers. At invoking the Air Elementals take a garter (*piece of lingerie used by women on their wedding day*), and put it in the circles´ intersection until the candles get consumed; later, clean the circles and names with the garter in order to impregnate it with the forces of the ritual and keep it in a safe place.

In the first-quarter phase, cut the garter halfway and sew it to a piece of clothing of the other without him or her noticing and remove it in the Full Moon night. Afterwards burn the two halves with a blue candle, throw the ashes to the wind at the first sunlight hour of the next Sunday of the Full Moon phase (*invoke the Air Elementals just like for the other rituals*).

• **Forgetting:** Light a white candle and write backwards (*mirror effect*) on it the name of the person from top to bottom, place it in the middle of two mirrors, so that, you can read the name the right in the mirrors' reflection. Practice this ritual in the last-quarter phase on Saturday at the first sunlight hour. Bury the remaining wax in a bare soil (*sand, desert, dry land, stones, etc.*)

• **The Aura's Force:** The Fire Element symbolizes passion, it is the force of desire and its presence increases love; magic doesn't oblige anybody to feel love, magic just attracts free and real feelings. Taking a bath under the Fire influence turns on our internal light and we will attract everything that is compatible with our personal vibration.

This formula has to be done during the first- quarter phase days.

You need to use 2 red candles, put one of them in front of you and the other one behind, both of them with some red rose petals; light the candles and stay up in the place for six minutes keeping the light around you. Candles don't get totally consumed because you will need them to enlarge your own aura.

At finishing the ritual, take the petals and put them underneath your sheet in order to receive their vibrations during night; if you light the candles during a storm, the power of love will be yours and you will attract a new and different force. When petals get withered, keep them in a vase with water and every morning rub yourself whit them after taking your daily shower.

This ritual is stronger if you practice it during spring, every first-quarter night.

• **Spark of Love:** This ritual works to influence an absent person, use a picture of his or hers to realize the sortilege; light two candles (white and blue), put them in close proximity in order to mix all the wax at melting.

When extinguishing the flames, take the remaining wax and keep it until meeting each other, at that moment take the spark of love with your left hand and pass it along your beloved´s back, you will see the results. If you also want to increase love, practice another ritual melting a few of this wax and **pronouncing this spell:**

«By the time we meet again,
Charmed you will become
And never, never again...
You will leave my love»

To Protect Energies

• Moon's Mirror:

You will need:

- 1 black candle
- 7 bitter plants
- 7 sweet plants
- 7 different seeds
- 7 green candles
- Amber oil
- 1 tablespoon of salt
- 1 moon's mirror

Procedure: To get the moon's mirror: find a round mirror (*not a magnifying one*) and put it in a place to receive the Full Moon's influence for three consecutive nights, being careful of taking it out during day to protect it of getting sunlight.

Get a strand of hair and a nail from you or the person you want to influence to obtain abundance.

In the last-quarter night, prepare the following bath with the plants: Mix the bitter and the sweet plants in a pot with 2 litters of water and put it on to the heat.

Before boiling, add a tablespoon of salt and let the preparation stand for twenty minutes (*To extract the essence*), after this time put the seeds in the pot with your left hand.

Procedure: At the fifth rising hour, exorcise the place where you want to transmute energies. Place the mirror down with the reflexing side up, light a black candle in the middle and use it to light the seven green candles which surround the mirror; at lighting the last green candle, put the black candle off, put the strand of hair and the nail in the middle of the mirror (*remember that the pot with the plants has to be close to these objects*).

Invoke the Air Element and while pronouncing the invocation, submerge your hands and feet in the bowl with plants; take that moment to release your thinking and limitations (*rancor, ideas, feelings, etc.*).

Start walking back barefoot and sprinkle the remaining water with the plants around the place of the ritual as a symbolism to call on abundance. Keep the candles alight until consuming, pick up the mirror and keep it in a dark place to avoid sunlight contact.

At the first rising hour, put the amber oil on your skin from head to foot. Bury the remains from the bowl (*plants and seeds*) in a grass or open field away from home. Light a black candle every night until finishing them during the following seven nights after practicing the ritual. Give cereals to people in need for seven days (*one person a day is enough*).

• **Protection Shield:**

In a Full Moon night, place four candles with the elements colors in front of a mirror and invoke the Four Elements. Prepare a perfume with these products:

- Cosmetic or mineral oil
- Orange leaves or any other aromatic plant
- 7 gray or black feathers
- A piece of gold
- 7 wild flowers picked up in the last-quarter phase
- Cinnamon

Procedure: mix the ingredients in the oil and let the mixture in the open for one day and night in the New Moon to release the powers of the plants and gold. During the first Full Moon night, light the candles in front of the mirror on the altar and rub yourself with the oil from feet to head while invoking the Elementals of the four Elements. Wear yellow clothing or use sheets of the same color to sleep. Don't get in physical contact with people during the three days previous to this ceremony, otherwise, the incoming energy will be passed to the person you got in touch.

Every day, after taking a shower, keep your body wet and rub it with the oil; you will see amazing changes.

To attract the Full Moon's Power

Over time, a special respect and veneration have existed for the Full Moon and its influence over living beings; as well as it strengthens specific characteristics in animals, which human beings take advantage of, this way:

• Tiger (*Fire Element*) Strength and cleverness
• Dog (*Earth Element*) Nobleness and fidelity

- Birds (*Air Element*) Increasing of freedom and emancipation desires
- Fish (*Water Element*) Increasing of proliferation and tranquility

You will need:

- 7 river stones (*preferably picked up on the waxing moon*)
- 1 brown candle
- 1 ounce of Full Moon water
- 1 round mirror

Procedure: in a Full Moon Thursday or Friday night, at an odd hour (*7, 9 or 11 p.m.*) put the mirror surrounded by seven river stones in the open all night long to be influenced by the moon; at the same moment light the candle to attract the moon's energy.

Next morning, put the water on your body visualizing the benefits you desire (*proliferation, strength, etc.*). After taking the bath see yourself in the round mirror, getting harmonized and imagining the animal you want to unify with. From that night on, keep the mirror, stones and remaining wax of the candles to realize your petition last. Try to be calm and remember your petitions and wishes. Do your spell with the elements you want and mentioning the corresponding animal.

To attract positive energies for a place (commercial premise, house, etc.)

You will need:

- 7 different grains
- 7 yellow flowers
- 2 purple candles
- New Moon water
- 1 broom

On Tuesday or Friday in the first-quarter, put the yellow petals and the grains at the corners of your house at night.

The next morning at the crack of dawn, take the broom and sweep from the outside in, sweeping the petals and grains too. At finishing, light the two candles behind the front door (*if you live in a bedroom, do it inside of your bedroom*) and pronounce the following conjuring:

> *"Taer in en et es zada*
> *Pique cia y el de la posname*
> *Fusi aq se dan odui*
> *Clo de poraun el ab lader"*

Later, spill some water drops (*while the candles are consuming*) shaping a circle to the left side of the door and a triangle to the right side. Pick up the grains and petals to leave them in an open place.

To liberate you from a curse

When people have been unfairly victim of hex or course have the possibility of undoing it in order to get them free from that work. It is important to clarify that the person who does the action has to be directly the affected one; it doesn't work if it is done by another person.

You will need:

- 4 nails from a horseshoe
- 1 small piece of parchment
- 1 magnetized white candle
- 1 clay pot

In the third last-quarter night (*at an odd hour*) light the candle on the altar to illuminate the action you are about to perform.

Take one of the nails and heat it up to write backwards (a*s if it were a quill*) your name on the right side of the parchment.

On the other side of the parchment, write (*the right way*) the name of the person who uttered the curse. Under that name, write these words:

«Adet, Adonay, Cherub, Seraph,
Untie what already is tied»

Pierce the four ends of the parchment with the four nails and keep it in a safe place until the first Full Moon night, put the candle off and keep it.

In the Full Moon night (*in an open field*) light in the clay pot the same candle you kept and burn the parchment with it. Keep the nails until the next morning.

Go to a field or a park and walk barefoot on the ground or land to print your feet on it. After printing them, pound one nail in the middle of the right footprint, the second nail in the middle of the left footprint and the third one between both of them; bend the fourth nail's tip inwards and keep it with you.

Fifteen days after performing the operation, you must go to a field at night (*if the person who uttered the curse is still alive*) and throw backwards the nail you kept, pronouncing the name of the person and saying:

«No matter what you gave me,
I give you the same back».

If the person who uttered the curse is dead, you must do the operation close to the door of a cemetery (*It doesn't matter if the person was buried there*), give food to a person in need during the following seven days.

It is necessary for you to remember that this ritual will work only if the curse was unfairly proffered and you don't feel any rancor against the person, on the contrary the ritual won't work.

• Energy Releasing Enchantment

Whenever you get objects from other people (*gifts, donations, purchasing*) or objects pawned or lent by you for any reason, have to know that they are infested and without noticing it, those energies might influence your life and projects (*business, work, love and family*).

Start working in the last-quarter night; about 9 p.m. Put a glass of water in the open to be influenced by the moon. Take some drops of your first urine at the first rising hour and mix them with the water. Put this preparation in a place away from the sunlight.

The same day, about 6 p.m. mix the preparation with some more water and use it to clean the objects (*It has to be in a sunless place*) with a white cloth.

Quick formulas

• **Chasing away envy:** To combat working discord, there´s nothing better than a blue candle on Friday at 9 p.m.

Being naked and barefoot, light the candle and take it with your right hand to pass it over your body (*beginning on the left side and finishing on the right side from feet to head*). This is a symbolism to clean aura, later, sitting in the lotus position, look at the candle while invoking the Elements, before the candle is consumed, look at yourself in a mirror bathed in light.

You will see immediately changes of other people's attitude.

After this sortilege, be calm and isolated during the following seven days. Light yellow candles every Wednesday at the first sunlight hour to maintain a harmonized environment.

• **Protection against evil energies:** First of all, practice an exorcism as previously explained. To avoid evil energies, have a white flowers arrangement, preferably roses; light them at night with white candles, the power of the Fire Element will annul evil energies which could be harmful. If roses whither, you will need three used candles from a baptism or some candles irradiated by happiness energy, place a mirror reflecting your front door and light the candles in a middle point as a protection in a Full Moon night.

• **Chasing away annoying people:** Light a white candle with the symbols of the Angels of the Four Cardinal Points and stick it in a crystal glass with its wax, fill it with water halfway down and let the candle consuming until getting off by the water; when that happens, invoke the Air and Water Elements pronouncing the name of the annoying person; upon finishing throw the water to the wind and bury the piece of candle and the glass in a field or meadow.

• **Protecting the house against evil energies:** In the last waning moon night or in the New Moon, practice an exorcism invoking the Elements.

On Monday on the second rising hour, burn incense and a cigar to impregnate the house's corners; light nine black candles shaping a square and invoke the Elements (*considering the four points*).

Let the candles totally consume as well as the cigar; wait until the first-quarter phase to spread rice or another grain around the house and the next morning, at dawn before the first ray of the sun appears, sweep the house from the inside out and give the grains to the birds.

Purifying the environment when misfortune has come: Place three yellow fruits in a central point of home for three days, and depending on the state they are after the three days proceed as follows:

• If fruits are rotten: exorcise the place and clean it with a bath of bitter plants.

• If fruits are black and hard: burn some aromatic plants, light 16 candles (*4 red, 4 green, 4 blue and 4 yellow*); it has to be done on Friday at the first setting hour, remember to invoke the Nature Spirits (*see the Grimoire*).

• If fruits remain the same: It means that you are in an ideal place to live. Increase positive energies lighting 3 white candles and doing 72 little rice circles around the house; leave the circles there.

At finding a new place to live in; get in walking backwards and barefoot, holding a yellow fruit with many seeds; take some rice and the seeds (*after eating the fruit*) and bury them in a flowerpot or spread them around the house before moving in.

• Neutralize energies after having a discussion: Prepare cinnamon incense and burn it for three consecutive days beginning on Tuesday during the last-quarter phase at the third setting hour. Moreover, light pink candles for seven consecutive days in the dining room at dinner.

To balance the environment in the place of residence: This ritual has to be practiced in a Full Moon Sunday at the first setting hour.

Put a round mirror on the floor behind your front door and a cut lemon (*cross-shaped*) on it while invoking the Fire, Earth, Air and Water Elementals; light 9 black candles surrounding the mirror and let them totally consume. At getting the candles totally consumed, take the objects and bury the lemon with the remaining wax of the candles in a field away from home, and throw the mirror backwards to a river without looking at the place where it fell; if you prefer may leave it on the shore of the river.

For Health

• With White Flowers

This operation will help you to get your health wishes potentiated by the Air Element, represented by the white flowers and the Full Moon. At Full Moon night get these elements:

- 3 white flowers (*daisy, roses, etc.*)
- 1 round mirror
- 1 white candle

Procedure: at 9 p.m. the same day, put three flowers on the mirror shaping a triangle and light the candle in the middle of it for fifteen minutes and focusing on your wish. Put the candle off and take one of the flowers to put it in the right pocket of a piece of clothing you wore that day (*blazer, pants, etc.*), put the second flower in the left pocket and the third one on your bedroom's door.

The next morning, take the three flowers and put them under your bed, keeping them right there until the next Full Moon phase when you have to take them out and throw to flowing water (*stream, river, current, etc.*), this is in order to chase illness and disease away from you.

Keep the candle to light it every night for fifteen minutes until it is totally consumed (*it is not important the number of nights the candle lasts*).

• River Stones in the New Moon

During this phase of the moon, the powers of the Fire and its benefits irradiate health and power.

You will need:

- 1 gold-pointed needle
- Yellow thread
- 3 little river stones

Procedure: in a New Moon night, at an odd hour, sew a river stone on a piece of clothing belonging to the ill person (*you or another person*) with the yellow thread and the needle.

Put another river stone under your bed (*or the ill person's bed*) and the other one, in the doorframe of the bedroom.

Conserve the river stones (*including the one on the piece of clothing*) for seven days and nights where you put them; after that, take them out and leave them in an open place (*park, field*) to come back to nature, and so on health reestablishes.

• **Magnetite "The Natural Magnet"**

As well as personal energy harmonizes with nature, health gets better.

You will need:

- A little water from the last-quarter phase
- Magnetite (*natural magnet from earth*)
- 1 white candle
- 14 leaves from a sweet plant

Procedure: In a last-quarter Friday night, mix in a bowl the water, the leaves and the magnetite and put the mixture in the open. Light the candle for one hour in the ill person's bedroom, and so on for the following nights until the candle is totally consumed.

On Saturday morning, put a little bit of water on the ill person's feet. From that day put the magnetite underneath his or her pillow to irradiate energy while sleeping.

Put this water with the leaves on the ill person's feet until finishing the preparation; this way, nature will reactivate energies to help improving his or her health.

• **Water to harmonize health**

You will need:

- A bowl with 2 liters of water
- 7 sweet plants
- 1 silver object and 1 gold object (*ring, pendant, earing, etc.*)
- 3 yellow candles

Procedure: in a New Moon on Saturday, at the first rising hour, mix the plants and the objects in the water and put the bowl in the open for a day and night. Form a triangle with the candles around the bowl and light them.

The next morning, strain the water and put it on the ill person's skin to harmonize his or her bioenergy fields with the influence of day and night.

• Conjuring of the sweet honey of Air

It's practiced in the last-quarter phase nights and **you will need:**

* River water, collected counter-current in a last-quarter night
* 7 different sweet plants
* Honey
* 7 white plants
* Clay or mud
* 1 mirror

Procedure: Mix in a pot the water, plants and honey on the altar; put the pot on to the heat until the plants release their essence; after doing that, light the candles on the altar in a circle clockwise and put the mirror and the clay or mud in the middle of it for five minutes.

Take the clay or mud and on a piece of clothing belonging to the ill person, knead it and moisten it with the water previously prepared. Mold a human figure with the person's characteristics which will be impregnated with his or her humor or bioenergy outpours. Let the figure on the mirror to be influenced by the moon and the candle light. The next day, put the figure at the foot of the ill person's bed while saying the following invocation:

For the power of the Air and Fire,
For the power of the Earth and water,
Spirits of the light,
I (say your name) invoke you
To become into reality my wish
Of healing this creature of nature
Healing his/her body, mind and soul
Pronouncing the magical words
Which you have duty of obedience with.

Han sagem
Han sagim
El ectinet se fur
Sol de igass
That everything I wish
Becomes into reality here.

Keep the figure for 9 moons (*nine moon phases*) to reinforce the effect, during that time you will light a white candle every Friday at the first rising hour.

Such figure can be unmade the same way you made it, in the same moon phase and using the same water you used to elaborate it, melt it until returning to its initial shape and take it to a current or stream to give it back to nature.

• Energy Transmutation

You will need three white or black candles, one egg, a bowl with water from the Full Moon and a flowerpot with black soil.

In a first-quarter night put the candles shaping an inverted triangle (*the sharp end towards you*), put the flowerpot and the bowl with water and the egg in it, in the middle of the triangle; light the candles while reciting the respective invocations (*the four Elements*) and focus on your wish. Your mental mode is very important and even more if this is about healing.

Take the wet egg and get it close to the ill person on the affected area, do 10 circles counterclockwise avoiding touching the person, pass the egg along the entire body 3 centimeters away from the skin cleaning the auric field. At finishing, bury the egg in the flowerpot without breaking it, if that happens you will have to start over. Take the piece of clothing and wet it with water from the bowl to clean the skin. Finally, take that water and spill it on the flowerpot, put the candles off with black soil and bury them in the flowerpot too.

Seven days later, at the beginning of the Full Moon phase, about midnight, bury the flowerpot in a field away from the ill person's house. It is also possible to practice this ritual to help yourself.

• Healing

The Fire Element purifies, heals and clears life processes. Many healing formulas are done through magical rituals using yellow candles.

Procedure: During the last-quarter phase, take a piece of clothing belonging to the ill person and light the yellow candle within the circles of protection together with the piece of clothing. Invoke the salamanders and smoke the garment in the dead of midnight, then, rub it onto a field to magnetize it (*with the Earth Element*) while invoking the Fire and Earth Elements.

At next dawn, dress the ill person with that piece of clothing to allow an energy exchange; trespassing illness to the clothing will get that the force of Earth and the purification of Fire bring the power to reestablish health. Four days later, in the New Moon, practice the ritual again at the first rising hour, this time burning up the piece of clothing in the circle after reciting the Fire Element Invocation.

The circles must be spacious enough to perform with no risks; the ritual concludes at burning up the piece of clothing. At dawn, throw backwards the ashes to the wind without looking back and pronounce your own spell.

It is important to clarify that these rituals will never replace a visit to the doctor; this is just an extra resource. Seek advice from a physician; it is your own responsibility to take into account some different points of view with regard to your wellness.

• Health Spells

Healing with Virgin Soil

Nothing better for healing than the Earth Element; it renews, regenerates and transmutes.

You will need:

- A piece of clothing (*of the ill person*)
- Virgin Soil (*clay or mud*)
- Water from the last-quarter phase

Procedure: Practice this ritual in the last-quarter phase about 3 p.m.; put the piece of clothing and the virgin soil within the circles of protection and invoke the Elements. Put your hands over the piece of clothing and invoke the Spirits of Nature (*see the Grimoire*). Put the piece of clothing and the virgin soil in the open to be influenced by the moon and before the sun rises keep them in a green fabric bag. Put a poultice of virgin soil on the affected area and rub it with the piece of clothing leaving it all night long. The next morning, bathe the patient with water from the last-quarter phase.

There's nothing useless in nature, we may access to a wide range of natural remedies with plants, greatly beneficial in a large majority. During Magick rituals in a state of deep meditation, you can ask for wisdom to know the plants which help you to mitigate a specific illness. That's what healers do in the jungle, they let themselves mentally go to be guided by magical beings and feel the power of medicinal plants.

In some cases, virgin soil consumption after practicing the ritual produces immediate healing.

• Health Conjuration

The Air Element symbolizes the divine breath, the onset of life, the first breathing, the newborn's sobbing, and consequently it has the force of life to be used in Magick as the healer breath.

You will need:

- Incense
- 3 white candles
- A piece of clothing (*belonging to the ill person*)
- Water from the Full Moon
- 1 cigar

Procedure: Burn the incenses within the circles of protection; get a cigar to work releasing the patient from the illness. At midnight take a piece of clothing of the patient or if possible the ill person itself and light the three candles around him or her forming a triangle with them; at the same time the incense burns, spill water from the Full Moon on the piece of clothing or patient, smoke the cigar on the piece of clothing or patient while invoking the Air Element and then pronounce a spell created by you.

Upon finishing, put the incenses and candles off very respectfully; from then on, the images of your mind must not be about illness but of health.

Continue with this ritual for nine consecutive days. Remember this: it is possible that the patient may lose its consciousness the first day of the ritual and fall into a deep sleep due to the beginning of this cleaning work.

Afterwards, you will begin a similar ritual taking an object belonging to the ill person, offering to the moon and incensing it, as cleaning the object the person is being released from the illness.

• Healing with Fire Sand

The influence of the first-quarter phase becomes water into a powerful Element. This is the time when aquatic bodies *"increase"* their power, being the moment to perform healing rituals. Light four candles (*green, blue, red and white*) forming a square within the circles of protection and make two more circles in the middle with fire sand. The water you will use for healing must be within the square. Practice this ritual the third day of the first-quarter at 9 p.m.; if the patient is absent, use an unwashed piece of clothing or sheet belonging to the same, put it under the bowl with water while invoking the Water Element.

Bring your hands close to the bowl and move them upside down to magnetize the water. The moon will be in charge of raising the water level which in turn will be ready to heal. The images in the operator's mind have to irradiate love and visualizing its wish coming true; while visualizing recite your own spell.

After saying the conjuring proceed as follows: put the candles off in the water and add small parts of fire sand; cover the bowl and the next morning bathe the patient with this water applying it with the wet piece of clothing, then get him or her dressed in white. Burn the used piece of clothing. Drinking water from reservoirs during in first-quarter nights brings the power of restoring as physically as mentally; sortileges are not necessary to carry out this formula. You may find the formula of abundance at combining rituals.

Quick Formulas

• **To increase your mental faculties:** Light three candles forming a triangle and put a crystal glass full of water in the middle, sit in front of it with the rim at eye level. Get focused looking at the water until seeing a kind of fog, at that moment invoke the forces of the Elements; that way you will acquire great skills of extrasensory perception, releasing from the subconscious mind the latent power inside of you.

• **To relieve pain:** Light a tallow candle invoking the Air Element and pass it over the affected area making circles counterclockwise. With the candle on, bring your hands close to the area in pain without touching it, take the melted tallow being careful of burning yourself and as soon as it gets cold, put it as a heating pad invoking the Water Element.

THE GREATEST WITCHCRAFT RITUALS

There are some special ceremonies which increase the energies of cosmos; they are celebrated on certain dates with a great planetary force. Have quiet, peaceful and harmonic thoughts and wishes to practice these rituals, this way abundance will come to your life; otherwise, if you are anxious or have a fixed idea, the effect will be the opposite and you will chase away positive energy.

Have your spells ready soon enough; these rituals are more powerful if are collectively practiced.

• Winter Solstice

This ritual is based on millenary techniques and knowledge from the Celtic culture using a mixture of water and essences as a representation of the regent Element. The meaning purpose is purifying to reach greater success in life, personal relationships, etc. awakening your skills of creating and experiencing the interior infinity; likewise, attracting happiness, magnetizing your body and including love to every action in daily life.

You will need:

- 1 blue candle
- Conjured Oil
- 7 sweet plants
- 7 red roses
- 1 clay pot
- 2 liters of water from the first-quarter phase

Procedure: this ritual is practiced on the 23rd of December, date corresponding to the Winter Solstice. After 7 p.m. put the 2 litters of water, the plants and red rose petals in the clay pot; leave the preparation in the open under moon influence (*close to a window or* *if possible in a courtyard or terrace).* The next morning after taking your daily shower, bathe your body with this filter, dress yourself without drying with a towel.

The following night, light the candle until totally consume; while the candle is lighting put the oil on your body massaging.

• Spring Equinox

It is the 23rd of March, this day the forces of the spring and the Earth's energy increase.

Over time, the spring has represented the beginning of new stages for human beings; it is the life reborn to new chances. In order to renovate and find new opportunities, we use energies emanated by nature.

You will need:

• Amber oil
• 1 green candle
• 3 sweet plants
• 3 seeds of a yellow fruit (previously influenced by the New Moon for three nights)
• 1 white candle

• A bowl with 2 liters of water from the first-quarter phase.

• 1 silver object and 1 gold object (*ring, brooch, pendant, earing, etc.*)

Procedure: the 23rd of March at night, put the gold and silver objects, the candles, plants, seeds and also add some amber oil in the bowl with water. The next morning take the candles and the gold and silver objects out; keep the water with oil, plants and seeds to take a bath later. Get a pair of your shinier shoes and put the gold object in the right one and the silver object in the left one. Put the pair of shoes in a place where they can be influenced by the moon.

While pronouncing the Earth Prayer light the candles close to the pair of shoes and let them consume totally; afterwards pick up the remaining wax and keep it. If one of the candles gets off itself, it is not necessary to light it again.

• Summer Solstice

The energetic and cosmic power of the 23rd of June has been known over time, it's the longest day of the year, the Summer Solstice. Solstices represent the time when the sun gets its maximum elongation in Equator to the North or to the South.

Since ancient times, it has been known that the Earth, Air, Water and Fire Elements awake during this night and join powers to disclose their secrets, increasing abundance.

Before midnight, the Elements make presence nesting in certain seeds and filtering in their natural oils. Legends state that the male fern seed gains magical energy during this special night.

You will need:

• Conjured oil
• Male fern seeds (*5 approximately*)
• 3 river stones
• 1 red candle
• 1 blue candle
• 7 wild flowers
• 1 quartz crystal, diamond, zirconium or any prism that discomposes the solar rays.
• A bowl (*bowl, platter, etc.*)
• 1 mirror
• Clay

Procedure: make a human figure with clay and bathe it with solar energy through the prism. In a Full Moon night at the first setting hour, draw the four symbols of the Princes of the Elements on a parchment (*See the symbols in the Grimoire*).

Sitting naked and facing the East, take the symbols and invoke the Spirits of Nature; take the prism allowing light to discompose through it and see the sparkles reflected on your body and eyes; look at the colors (*green, red and blue*) allowing the rays to move playing on your skin and try at the same time to mold the clay while everything is being influenced. The place has to be semi-dark, getting only one beam of light to focus on it in order to receive the sun influence.

Summer Solstice is the longest day and the shortest nigh of the year and it's also called Saint John's Eve. Clay influenced by the sun represents the beginning of the life. At this time you will need to have a bowl with water and flowers aroma (*it can be petals*) to unify the clay with the Four Elements.

An ancient legend states that people performed miracles making a clay figure and giving energetic life to it, its name was GOLEM. If you want to try it, write the word EMET on the figure's forehead to impregnate it of your personal outpour. Several testimonies said that the figure came into life and grew up depending on the increasing of psychic energy irradiated by the practitioner of this ceremony.

Six months later. On the Winter Solstice (*23rd of December*), erase the first letter "*E*" from the figure's forehead, having as a result the word "*MET*", the accumulated energies will give you abundance for everything you want and a great power. Remember, this figure is a representation of yourself, at elaborating it you must do a hole in its chest to put a blood drop from you, extracted in a Full Moon night from the middle finger of your left hand, as well as a hair and a piece of nail. The rest of the body has to be drawn the best way to make it as similar as possible to you; finally cover it with a green cloth as a protection against evil influences. The figure, while holding your energy, will channel every event that comes for you, liberating you from evil influxes. Keep it close to you at practicing rituals, any parasite energy will be received by it, at the same time that you make more sortileges, its power will increase until getting the point of materializing your wishes through this figure.

When the figure breaks down because it has a lot of accumulated evil energy or caused by force majeure, at the beginning of the New Moon at the seventh setting hour, erase the word *"MET"* from its forehead and unmake it in a bowl with water until the figure becomes into clay.

• Fall Equinox

Nature during its constant evolution manifests its power to the human beings in order to take advantage of those energetic forces for their own benefit. Those forces denominated *"subtle energies"* have been known throughout history with many other names; personalities like King Solomon used this knowledge learning the art of invoking them for his benefit.

You will need:

• 4 candles representing the Elements (*red, green, blue, white*)
• Autumn fragrance
• Incense with a tree fragrance (*pine, cedar, etc.*)
• 1 egg
• Cedar sticks or a piece of cedar trunk

Procedure: Put the four candles shaping a square on the altar (*it is not important the position of each color*), put a bowl with water in the middle of the candles and deposit in it the incense with the cedar sticks, the egg and the autumn fragrance. Light the red candle with your right hand and use this candle to light the rest of them, pronounce the Air Element invocation followed by your own spell and let the candles on.

Take the egg with the right hand and carefully rub your body upside down cleaning stranger energies from it. You can feel fainting or dizzy, that's normal; you can also experience different sensations at cleaning your body. The next day, bury the egg in a field away from home before sunrise.

Important: if the egg breaks, the energies taken from your body will come back to you, it is recommended to cover the egg with a black cloth to protect it. At finishing, lay down for twenty minutes leaving your mind quiet.

There's something about this ritual you should bear in mind, while laying down you might experience an "*astral projection*" (*an experience out of your physical body*), getting to feel that the Air Elementals communicate with you through several ways. Afterwards, put the candles off, use the remaining to light them one by one the following nights regardless of the color, until they are totally consumed.

The next morning (*after practicing the ritual*) use the fragrance on your body and take a shower. Burn the incense and the cedar sticks.

• New Year's Ritual

Psychic energy accumulates every 31st of December before midnight is irradiated by millions of people feeling wellness wishes and mental emanations of success for the next year; it is very rare to find a person projecting evil or destructive energies at that moment.

This is a unique moment; happiness, optimism, the wish of a better future and leaving the past behind create a specific energy that can be channeled and accumulated to be used during the next year applying an ancient ritual letting free a little bit of the preparation every month; this way, we will have the forces of the last night of the past year during the twelve months of the new year.

It is important to clarify that this is a personal and individual ritual, if you share its elements, the enchanted energy including yours will be projected to the person you decided to share this with; therefore, you will receive the consequences of your actions. For that reason, at the moment of practicing the ritual, your thoughts must be focused on yourself and nobody else. If you want to protect your family with this energy, only getting personally the influence you will benefit them, it is not necessary thinking of them at that moment.

You will need:

- 1 white wine or champagne bottle
- 12 sprigs of wheat (*with grain*)
- 12 yellow candles
- Love oil
- 3 seeds of a yellow fruit

Candles symbolize the light, the sprigs of wheat symbolize abundance and the wine or champagne symbolize happiness and they will be the path to triumph.

Procedure: At a quarter to midnight on the 31st of December, find a place to be alone (*bedroom, bathroom, living room, field, etc.*) make a circle counterclockwise starting at twelve o'clock (12, 11, 10, 9, 8, 7...) with the twelve candles putting them with the left hand and staying into the circle; shape a triangle with the wheat sprigs (*4 sprigs on each side*) and put the three seeds in the middle.

Put the champagne in a bowl and place it next to the triangle into the circle, and at five minutes to twelve, light the candles clockwise starting at twelve o'clock (12, 1, 2, 3, 4...).

At twelve o'clock recite the invocation of the Spirits of Nature; at the same time imagine whatever you wish, for example: quietness, happiness, health, prosperity, etc. mix in a bowl the champagne with some Love Oil and recite your own spell to express your wishes for the next year.

With your right hand and in the same direction you previously put them, pick up the candles and the sprigs to submerge them in the wine or champagne. Repack the champagne in the bottle, keep the candles, the seeds already magnetize and leave the wheat sprigs to dry in the sun.

The first of January between 5 and 8 a.m. light a yellow candle and let it consume. The same day, take the grains from one of the wheat sprigs and give them as a present to different people. Shake the champagne and take a little to rub your entire body with it, the champagne has to last for the 12 months of the year in order to make the ritual the first day of each month to release the psychic energy taken from the last 31st of December.

Note: The 1st, 2nd and 3rd days of January burn in the morning (*no matter what time it is*) the incenses one a day. Keep the seeds in a white fabric bag within your personal things throughout the year.

• Tuesday 13th

This date happens twice or three times a year, it is special to release negative energies that can be affecting places and people.

You will need:

- Fire sand
- Essence of the Magical Beings
- 1 yellow candle
- 7 different wild flowers
- Orange peels, previously dried in sun for three days
- 7 cinnamon sticks
- 2 white feathers

Procedure: on Monday 12th a 7 p.m., put 2 liters of water from a current in a bowl and mix it with the essence, add the wild flowers petals, the cinnamon sticks and the orange peels; place the preparation in a place where it can be influenced by the moon until next day, then keep it away from sunlight.

On Tuesday 13th after 7 p.m. filter the water and take a bath with it.

At that time, the yellow candle has to be lit in the place where you are to illuminate the moment when essences and aromas touch your skin. After bathing, put the candle off to keep the remaining to light it the following night.

The next day, after taking a shower, go to a place where the wind blows (*window, terrace, field, park*) and holding a feather on each hand in a meditative attitude, think of two special petitions, blow first to heaven the feather on your right hand and think about your wish while it is flying, do the same operation with the other feather. Afterwards, spread Fire Sand surrounding your house starting on the right side of the front door (you must be facing the house from the outside) and finishing on the left side of the front door. Leave the Fire sand to be spread and taken by the time.

Caution: Commercial essences may contain alcohol which in turn, may releases flammable gases. Keep a prudent distance between essences and candles to avoid an accident.

• Friday 13th

Within Wicca's wisdom and occultism exists the tradition of practicing cleansing rituals on Friday 13th. The legend states this is a unique day that due to the time and Earth position stops the flow of energy; as a consequence, many different events might come up. It is an ideal date to cleanse your life and home from negative energies. Practice the ritual as follows:

First Part

Wear in white (*blouse, pants, sweater, shirt, etc.*). Select the objects you want to throw out or those which cause pain (*pictures, letters or any old items*).

Some people prefer writing those situations they desire to chase away from their lives (*illness, poorness, feelings, etc.*).

On the eve of the 12th, leave a yellow fruit that contains seeds (*orange, papaya, melon*) in the open.

On Friday 13th in the morning, get out from your house backwards and carrying the items you will dispose of and the fruit, leave everything in the garbage, eat the fruit and keep the seeds; get in the house backwards and place the seeds on the floor behind the front door after putting them in a bag to avoid losing.

Second Part

You will need:

- Fire Sand
- 1 white candle
- Perfume of stars

On Friday 13th after 7 p.m. put some fire sand in different places of the house from right to left and from the door to inside.

Note: we recommend putting the fire sand on pieces of paper to pick it up easier.

Place the perfume and the candle separated at the corners of a private room (*bathroom, bedroom, etc.*), light the candle with the right hand and recite the Fire Element Invocation.

Meditate about the positive things you want to attract only for you. Let the candle alight until finishing. The next day, use a half perfume to bathe yourself and the other half for cleaning home the same day. Before doing that, pick up the fire sand and leave it in an open place (*field, meadow, park, etc.*).

- **Holly Week Friday**

(Energy Transmutation)

This date has had a special symbolism; energetic polypsychism comes out allowing expert people in magic to draw on it. Most people experience personal changes and regret. Such energies can be channeled to realize your wishes and petitions.

You will need:

- 3 bitter plants
- The Symbols of the Princes of the Four Elements
- 1 white candle
- 1 black candle
- 1 egg (*no matters the color and hopefully, it hasn't been refrigerated*)
- 7 sweet plants
- 1 glass of water

Procedure: On Friday before 7 a.m. clean your house as follows: Put 3 bitter plants in a bowl with 2 liters of boiling water as an infusion; use it to clean the entire house (*including floor, doors, windows and furniture*). About 3 p.m. light a white candle and take the egg with your right hand to pass it all over your body (*without touching it*) from foot on the left side to head; make a circle counterclockwise over the forehead and take the egg with your left hand to make another circle over the forehead again but clockwise this time; now, pass the egg all over your body on the right side to feet. Upon finishing, break the egg and put it in the glass of water under your bed, let it there until Sunday at 3 p.m.

Clean the house on Sunday (*this day symbolizes resurrection*) with an infusion of the 7 sweet plants. At 3 p.m. pour the content of the glass (*water and egg*) in a current of water. That very Sunday at night, draw with gold ink on a parchment the Symbols of the Four Princes (*Seraph, Cherub, Tharsis and Ariel*) which you can find at the end of this book. Later, light the black candle and burn the parchment in a meditative attitude while seen the ashes spread by the wind.

• SAMHAIN (Ritual of the 31st of October)

This is the most important date since the Celtic Culture times; it was considered the end and beginning of the year. People used to invoke the Elements, Nature and

Stars to express gratitude and make petitions for the incoming times.

This ceremony is held on October 31st in an even hour at night (8, 10 or 12). It is recommended to wear white.

You will need:

• The Cauldron of the Magical Beings (*with plants and aromas*)
• 1 white candle
• Fire sand
• 12 seed or 12 grains of cereals
• 1 mirror

Procedure: The night of the 31st you must be barefoot and in a meditative attitude to form the following shape:

Make a wide circle clockwise with the 12 grains around the mirror, draw a triangle with fire sand on the mirror and put the cauldron and the lit candle within the triangle.

Recite the prayer as follows:

Oh, great and powerful Jupiter,
I come to you finding your friendship,
Your emissaries bring to me
Rich and soft spirits.

Spirits of Nature
Sent by Jove
Your pal who I love.

Thank you for your generosity
And close friendship,
Great Spirit! Your rich and sincere participation
In friendship I implore you
For prosperity to descend over me
Thanking you wholeheartedly,
My own light is now shinier
Seeing splendid and rich greenery everywhere
Good luck is the law of my life.
So be it.

Straight away (*keep in mind the white candle has to be lit*), in case of having a special petition (*may be to help another person*), recite the following prayer:

For the power of the magical beings,
gnomes and fairies,
I invoke this wish tonight
(*pronounce your wish*)

I want it to be real for
(*your name or the other person's*)
At burning the plants
For light and darkness,
Everything becomes into brightness
Rami, enab, eia, una
Te que sa un mopa
Treco, cafu, en la dan.

Note: The plants mentioned above are the same in the cauldron. If the candles are blown off, do not light them again. Leave the remains in an open place where the wind blows. Keep the mirror and the grains in a safe place and within the first five days of each month bury one of the grains out of home to germinate your wishes and prosperity and they can be stable throughout the year. Keep the cauldron in a safe place too.

CHAPTER V

GRIMOIRE OF INVOCATIONS

«What's done is done, what's said is said»

Since immemorial time, wizards and witches have had communication with energies coming from angels and spirits of nature to obtain benefits for their power. Upon invoking them, we attract their presence that inundates with force our rituals.

Spells and enchantment in Magick are done verbally, The Word materializes thoughts. Pronounce these invocations decidedly and resolutely, never doubt, you own the power of contacting with magical energies.

Every wizard or witch creates prayers to contact with angelical forces which allow him or her accomplishing the great work of witchcraft.

As soon as you feel ready to do it, will create your own prayers; for a start, recite the following prayers, they are your first Witchcraft Grimoire, the initiated has started the path.

INVOCATIONS AND PRAYERS OF ELEMENTS AND ELEMENTALS

Fire Element

Blazing Fire, incessant and continuous power, spirit of everything who lives in everything, I invoke your presence at this time to illuminate my mind and my world at the same time that the sun illuminates the minds of the entire world, may the eternal and powerful force of creation be in my mind now and forever.

Oh, blazing Fire!
Shining and enduring within yourself,
And the pure splendor
Flows from your essence
In endless streams of light,
Nourishing your own spirit.

Infinite King of light,
Displace darkness from
The road of my life,
May your pure and infinite force
Transform my thought into reality,
Feed my soul with the endless wealth

Of the unlimited substance
To obtain spiritual and material things.
Djin, allow salamanders to become into reality
My wish at this altar of Fire
Where I invoke you
And if this is for me to advance
And grow spiritually
Make my wish come true.

Prayer to Salamanders

Eternal, ineffable and no created,
King and Father of everything,
You are ridden in the fast car of the worlds,
Those which unnecessarily spin,
Dominator of ethereal immensities
Where the throne of your power rises,
From the altitude which your penetrant eyes
Disclose everything,
And your holly ears,
Are hearing everything.
Attend to your beloved children
Since the beginning of the centuries,
Because your aureate, great and eternal majesty,
blazes all over the world,

Heaven and stars,
And you will rise over all of them.
Oh, blazing Fire!
Shining and enduring within yourself,
By your own splendor
And endless streams of light
Flow from your essence
To feed your infinite spirit.

This infinite spirit nourishes everything
And creates this endless treasure of substance
Always disposed for the generation who
makes it And takes over the shapes
That you inspired since the beginning.

From this spirit also come
Those holly Kings who encircle your throne
And are parts of your court.

Oh, Universal Father! Oh, Unique!
Oh, Father of the blessed ones!
Mortals and immortals!
You have created wonderful substances

Similar to your eternal thinking,
And your adorable essence.

You have conceded
Superiority to the angels,
Those who announce your true to the world.
Anyways, you have created us
In the third category
Of your elemental empire.
Hence, our continuous preoccupation
is praising and adoring our designs.
Hence, we burn in the endless aspiration
Of possessing you.

Oh, Father! Oh, Mother! The loveliest mother!
Oh, admirable archetype of motherhood
And the purest love!
Oh, Son, the flower of the children!

Oh, shape of every shape:
Soul, Spirit, Harmony and
Number of everything!
Bless us!
Amen.

Earth Element

Earth, free and eternal and everything you do fulfill,
Incessant and continuous power,
Spirit of everything,
You may live in everything,
I invoke your presence at this time
To illuminate my mind and my world,
May the eternal and powerful force of creation
Be now and forever.
Oh, Earth that covers everything!
Hence, you cover everything and last in yourself.
Pure love flows from your essence,
In endless streams of life,
Nourishing your own spirit.

Infinite Queen of Earth and Nature,
Displace darkness from the road of my life,
And your pure and infinite force
Transform my thoughts into reality,
Feed my soul with the endless wealth
Of your unlimited substance
To obtain spiritual and material things.

Leprechauns,
Allow Magical Beings and Gnomes

To make my wish real,
At this altar where I invoke you
If it is for my advance and spiritual growing,
Become my wish into reality.

Magical Beings and Gnomes Prayer

Invisible King who took Earth as support,
You have opened abysses to swell them
By your omnipotence.
You, whose name makes the vaults of the world,
shake,
You, who makes the seven metals run
Through the veins of the Earth,
Monarch of the Seven Lights,
Remunerator of the underground workers,
Take us to the desirable Air
And to the kingdom of clarity.

We all staying up and working without rest,
Looking and waiting for the twelve stones
Of the Holly City,
For the buries treasures,
For the magnetic nail that
Goes through the center of the world.

Lord: have mercy of those who suffer,
Expand our chests, lift our heads up;
Make us greater, Oh Balance and Movement!

Oh, day involved in night!
Oh, darkness watched by the light!
Oh, argentine whiteness! Oh, golden splendor!
Oh, crown of living and melodious diamonds!

You, that who carries heaven on your finger
Like a sapphire ring,
You, that who hides the kingdom
Of gemstones underground,
The wonderful seed of the stars,
Live, Reign and be the eternal
Dispenser of that richness
Of which you have made us the guardians.
Help us!
Amen.

Air Element

Free and eternal Air,
Incessant and continuous power,
Spirit of everything,
You may live in everything,
I invoke your presence at this time
To illuminate my mind and my world,
At the same time that
The sun illuminates the minds of the world,
May the eternal and powerful
Force of creation
Be in my mind now and forever.

Oh, pure and serene Air!
Shining and enduring within yourself,
And the pure love
Flows from your essence
In endless streams of life,
nourishing your own spirit.

Infinite King of the Air,
Displace darkness from
The road of my life,
May your pure and infinite force
Transform my thoughts into reality,

Feed my soul with the endless wealth
Of the unlimited substance
To obtain spiritual and material things.

Paralda, allow sylphs, Sylphids and zephyrs
To become my wish real
At this altar
Where I invoke you
And if this is for me to advance
And grow spiritually
Make my wish come true.

Sylphs, Sylphids and Zephyrs Prayer

Spirit of Light, Spirit of Wisdom,
No created King, whose breathe gives and takes
The shape of every being,
You, that whom the life of everything the created
Is a changing shadow and a passing vapor
You, that who inhales and everything which
Gets out from you, comes on you.

Endless movement in eternal balance,
Be eternally blessed!

We all praise and bless you in the empire
Of created light, of the shadows,
Of reflexes and of images,
And incessantly, Aspire to your immutable
And undying clarity.

Let come to us
The light from your intelligence,
The warmth of your love.

So, that what is mobile, will be immobile,
The shadow will be a body,
The Air Spirit will be a soul,
And fantasy will be real.

We won't be crushed by the storm,
Because we all will retain
The bridles of, The winged horses of dawn
We all will run
The run of the night winds
To fly towards your presence.
Oh, creating breathe of every being!
In the flow and reflow of your eternal word,
Which is the divine ocean of movement,
Protect us!
Amen.

Water Element

Blazing Water, Incessant and continuous power,
Spirit of everything,
You may live in everything,
I invoke your presence at this time
To illuminate my mind and my world,
At the same time that
The sun illuminates the minds of the world,
May the eternal and powerful
Force of creation
Be in my mind now and forever.

Oh, pure and eternal Water!
Shining and enduring within yourself,
And the pure love, Flows from your essence
In endless streams of life,
Nourishing your own spirit.

Infinite King of the Water,
Displace darkness from, The road of my life,
May your pure and infinite force
Transform my thoughts into reality,
Feed my soul with the endless wealth
Of the unlimited substance
To obtain spiritual and material things.

Neckna, allow Undines, Nodites and Nereides
To become my wish real
At this altar
Where I invoke you
And if this is for me to advance
And grow spiritually
Make my wish come true.

Undines, Nodites and Nereides Prayer

Impetuous and terrible King of the sea,
You who have the keys of
the heaven's waterfalls
And enclose the underground waters
Deep inside the earth,

King of the flood and spring waters,
King of the torrential waters,
You who open springs
Of rivers and fonts,
You who send humidity,
Equivalent to the Earth's blood,
To the sage of the plants,
We adore you and invoke you.
Talk to us, Your mobile and instable creature,
In the middle of the greatest Sea commotions

We will tremble in front of your presence,
Talk to us, In the babbling of limpid waters
And we will be eager of your love.

Oh, immensity
In which every river of the being
Is going to get lost,
And incessantly reborn in you!
Oh, Ocean of infinite perfections!
Zenith contemplated in deepness!

Deepness exhaled by you on the highness,
Drive us to the real life, By intelligence and love!
Take us to immortality by sacrifice,
To get to be Worthy of someday offering you
The water that represents
Blood and tears to forgive mistakes.
Save us!
Amen.

Invocation of the Spirits of Nature

Little beings from anywhere,
I'm looking for your friendship and harmony,
Genie Gronky, listen to my call,
Leprechauns come to us,

Half gnome and half enchantment Force
Come to transmit us your festive humor.
Neckna and your mischievous Undines,
Play with us your old games.
Paralda, Zephyrs of the Air,
Take care of my skin while being naked,
Salamanders, leaded by Djin,
Play with the flames of the altar candles.

Spirits all of Nature,
Accept our friendship,
We all really want to be
An object of love for you,
Our souls are pure as you can see.

While you sing and play,
We see how our problems dissipate,
Your smile, affection and tenderness
Invade us, And help us to feel
as alive as you are.

Prayer to the Spirits of Nature

Oh, Spirits of light, Genies of Nature who settle
Celestial spaces, I (*Say your name*)
Invoke you at this solemn hour

To come at this little Altar of Fire
Which I have raised in your honor.

Genie Gronky,
Shower with your virtues this place.

Neckna,
Open your gold-bearing wings
Covering my house with them
To live happy.

Paralda,
Allow me to stay healthy.

Djin,
Deluge me with all kind of prosperities.

Leprechauns,
Give me your power of converting
My thoughts into reality.
Oh, Spirits of heavenly light,
Receive my offering,
For happiness, abundance and health
To reign in my life.

CONCLUSION AND SUGGESTIONS

You already have entered into a new universe; it is the moment for you to get a tittle as an Initiated in the Occult Sciences, there's no limits at practicing rituals, the knowledge latent in your mind is ready to flow, so don't be scared to be an adventurer and practice; keep your thoughts away from failure. You may fail at the beginning but remember that mistakes bring the experience you need to gain wisdom. There's a lot of formulas in magic which work through other kinds of arts but the Elements; this is the first page of the book of wisdom.

Ancient wizards knew the existence of this forces, but they didn't name them by the same confusing and strange names used today. You now possess knowledge enough to get into the path of magic, your own knowledge flows at discovering the answer to the question: Who are we? We highly recommend you these three magical words which open the door toward your desires: Willpower, Discipline and Constancy.

*The Master **Kadaisha** said:*

"Every being is a wizard, a Master and a Learner inside"

SECRETS FOR INITIATED WIZARDS AND WITCHES

Magic is only one; but it changes into different kinds of magic according to the intention, power is gestated in thoughts; it is very important to take into account the law of similarity, power increases inasmuch as the wizard or witch discovers the roads to the own inner being.

We already have advanced a section of the road and now you are ready for the magical keys, so let's go to receive the secrets; if you are on the road and find the flame of the power of Nature inside of you, Mannon will give you the force to realize whatever you want.

Magic represents the attraction of similar, and working with everything you have learned you will experience unexpected results; we have previously seen some rituals relatively easy to practice, we can call them *"Domestic Rituals"*, but now, we're going to know the Master Keys of Wicca. Remember that if one of your wishes or influences comes true, you can't regret or the influence will come back to you three times. In fact, it is very important thinking carefully what you want, likewise don't overindulge in ambition of money, that's a mistake very easy to make and you will pay an expensive price later, remember that sooner or later, magic comes back to its creator.

Never use magic with evil purposes, by contrast try to emanate thoughts of light and hope, be helpful instead of being a burden, don't be arrogant, don't be destructive, on the contrary, be transparent and serene; if you are a woman, learn how to be silent and patient; if you are a man, avoid being greedy and avaricious.

The following words are written for you to analyze, reflect on and draw conclusions; some excerpts are riddles, you have to discover the secret.

The thread of the witch is invisible, but it ties everything that has to be limited. (*Remember that Magic is the attraction of similar. What is the thread of the witch that ties and is invisible?*).

The thread works to get couples together, neutralize someone harmful, catch wishes, dominate someone mentally and everything related to "*having*".

Analyze, allow your mind to fly, just think: What is really what the thread catches?...

Antique keys which unlock doors are similar to liberation, but they also lock doors and that's similar to limitation. Depending on your intention the key becomes stronger to a side or another; if you want to unlock the door, the key turns right or if you want to lock the door the key turns left; think about all the things you can do with those keys.

Keys hanged on the front door as mobiles are amulets; they release and neutralize parasite energies.

Keys underneath the mattress or stabbing an object (*no hanging*) work as closures or limitations; be careful when using them that way.

You will realize there's a multitude of magical combinations, for example: making a mobile with only one key and a gold ring and hanging it at a corner of the house will open the door to money and abundance.

Let's do something... try 50 combinations using keys, I will help you:

1. We are going to hang two keys at the corner where the fabric of threads of the witches is, one of the keys has to be hanging from the hole and the other from the point; this will attract progress and protection.

2. We will find a little wooden crate to put in it your bad memories like pictures, letters, receipts, documents of debts, penal obligations, etc. (*all those things which represent problems*). We need two shackles to close the crate passing a key through them. We will practice this ritual invoking the Earth Element; within a few days you will amaze of seeing incredible events happening.

3. We will keep a diary key hanging from the neck for nine days, then we will make an abundance ritual to transfer our power to it; afterwards we are going to open a bank account and as soon as we receive the check book, we will open a little hole on the upper-right part (*think well what side you turn the key to*), you will notice how magically your economy increases. 27 days after, you are going to find the night trapped in day, and at perceiving the perfume of the yellow bells, you must take a coin or bill, open the door of the elves with the magical key to find a green stone, use it forever…

4. If you want to lose weight, hang three keys under your bed…

5. If you want to help an ill person to get better, hang a group of keys from the roof over the bed of the person, where are the keys supposed to turn?

Pictures are a physical and mental representation of people, the face shows feelings, observe some pictures and try to discover the mental state of each person.

You need to be careful; sometimes wishes are more powerful than reason, you might commit painful acts, and regret is worth nothing; magic has a great power to construct or destroy, that only depends on you and your wish.

Women have to be especially careful during the menstrual period; today, envy and selfishness are nestled in prejudiced minds; imagine the number of things that some people can do with your blood; do not leave it anywhere…

In the same way, we have to be careful with our hair, nails, and tears; if your tears fall into the hands of a black wizard, he can send too much pain to your life and surely you will realize it after a long time. To do a protection chain, you can give this manual to other people, it's a way to build a harmonious world learning magic.

Whenever you feel enchanted, take three drops from the candy of the Air and put them on your private parts… the magic imposed on you will disappear one day after…

The world of magic is unlimited, everything has a representation, everything is similar to something and everything has an upper and a back side, everything has two poles, everything is one with two ends. Love and hate are two extremes of the same feeling.

The mind is the creator and conductor of polarity and intention of the wizard or witch, so everything represents everything.

If you want to go deeper inside the sense of mind and magic read the book "*Knowledge for the Initiated*".

What do cloves represent?
What does a ring represent?
What does an eyelash represent?

What kind of magical ritual can I perform using a watch?

It would be impossible to finish this Grimoire if I mention the entire list of things you can do in magic, but you are not alone, thousands of people are connected by internet in a great magical coven; we don't speak about the Book of the Shadows anymore because there's a place for Wicca in every computer of the world.

GLOSARY

AGE OF THE MOON: Named synodic month and corresponds to the complete cycle of the Moon according to its four phases and is 29.53 days.

ALCHEMY: Arabic word that is the essence of magic, predecessor of modern chemistry. From its beginnings it was an occult practice belonging to hermetic schools. It tried to understand how nature worked to find metals transmutation. Paracelsus in the fifteenth century changed this conception, guiding it towards human benefit.

ALL HALLOWS EVE: The desire of the Catholic religion to Christianize the ritual of Samhain tried to change the celebration of this Sabbath for Saints' day. English phrase meaning *"All Hallows Eve"*, belongs to the Catholic tradition and is celebrated on October 31st. As time passed, it contracted to form the word Halloween.

APOGEE: Point where the Moon is farthest from the Earth.

BACO SABAS: God Dionysus (*Greek culture*). He was also known as Sabacios or Sabazios, normally, he is the God of wine, of happiness and joy, from him the name of Sabbath or festivity is revealed.

BELTANE: Important date in Wicca magic, it is the festival of love and sexuality, the Sabbath of the woman-man power is held on May 1st, the interval between the spring equinox and the summer solstice.

CABALA: Interpretive art that dates from the Hebrew culture, based on the vibrations of words and numbers, with what is sought to find out the future or hidden things. The cabal symbolizes mystical knowledge.

CAULDRON: Special container to burn perfumes and produce aromas.

CELTIC: Indo-Germanic people who emigrated in prehistoric times first to Central Europe and later to Gaul, Spain and the British Isles. The Celts were defeated and absorbed by the Romans. The remains of its culture have been best preserved in Brittany, Wales, Ireland and Galicia. Its culture was based on the knowledge of cosmos and the harmonization of nature, through rituals.

COVEN: Meeting of witches in which they worshiped Faun and Diana (*Gods of nature*). It is also known as the secret site for the practice of rituals.

CRESCENT: Phase Fourth Crescent, where the Moon is rising, with the tips up.

DANCE TO THE SUN: It is the period between 12 o'clock to 1 o'clock in the afternoon when the sun is at its most vertical point towards the earth and its greatest power is received.

DIANA: Goddess of nature, she was also known as Artemis.

DRUID: It is the caste of the priests of the Celtic culture.

EAST: Hours of the day when the sun begins its phase of appearance, and comprises between 12 a. m. until 6 a.m.

EFFLUVIUM: Generic term to designate the supposed emanation of energy or matter that comes from beings or things.

ELEMENTALS: Corresponds to the spirits of the elements of nature.

ELEMENTS: Are Fire, Earth, Air and Water.

ELVES: It is the elemental of the earth, governed by Leprechauns. They are fantastic beings, whose name comes from the goblin voice and in turn from the Celtic deneet (*domesticated, familiar*).

ENCHANTMENT: Set of inexplicable phenomena normally linked to a specific site, or to an action propitiated by one person towards another.

EQUINOX: Time when, because the Sun is over the equator, the days are equal to the night in all the earth, and this is verified annually from March 20th to 21st and from September 22nd to 23rd.

ESBAT: It is the informal meetings of the witches that can be weekly, biweekly, monthly. They are the rituals that are executed in the different phases of the moon, and the different phases of ovulation.

EXTINGUISHER: Instrument used in rituals, is used to drown the fire of the candles. It has a long handle and ends in a bell shape.

FAUN: Among the beliefs of Wicca witchcraft, it is symbolized as the father of nature.

FILTER: It is a preparation based on water, oil and natural products for specific use.

FULL MOON: Abbreviation of the Full Moon Phase.

GEOCOSMOBIOLOGY: New science that studies the electromagnetic influence of the planets and the earth in humans.

GNOMES: It is the elemental of the earth, governed by Leprechauns.

GOECIA: It is the equivalent of Black Magic.

GRIMOIRE: It is the magic manual or breviary. This name is derived from the French voice *"grimoire"*, which in turn comes from the Latin *"gramma"* which means letter, sign, revelation.

HALLOWEEN: According to the Celtic culture, this date, October 31st was the last day of the year, where spirits and other supernatural beings were free, it was also the propitious day to guess about the New Year.

HERMETIC: Relative to the teachings of Hermes. Knowledge that, being managed by small groups of people, remained almost hidden. It is a synonym of closed.

KADAISHA: He is a monk of the Shamballah temple, who is in charge of being the guide in the discovery and harmonization of the forces of the cosmos and of his own interior.

KYBALION: It is the set of seven fundamental laws of nature attributed to Hermes Trismegistus, which are found in the Emerald Table.

LYCANTHROPY: It is called to the fact of unification with energies of nature, which causes a man to transform into a wolf, or the equivalent in behavior.

MAGNETISM: It is defined as the influence that a person can have over another, or over something. It comes from

Franz Anton Mesmer, who talked about the fluids of each person and how they affected or cured others.

MAGNETIZE: Radiate something with some special energy, either from a person, or a star.

MELTING POT: Container to melt products at different temperatures.

MOON PHASE: They are the different successive aspects that happen to the Moon, and it is Waning, New, Crescent and Full.

NEREIDAS: Elemental of water, ruled by Necna.

NODITAS: Elemental of water, ruled by Necna

NOVILUNIO: Abbreviation of the New Moon Phase.

PERIGEE: It is that point in the path of the moon that is closest to the earth.

PHALLIC: Related to the phallus, ancient ritual for fertility.

POTION: Special cooking with high magical content, is based on different plants according to the need.

PSI: Acronym or abbreviation with which are designated to the parapsychological phenomena, and are divided into: subjective or psychic phenomena (*Psi-Gamma*) and objective or specific phenomena (*Psi-Kappa*).

SABBATH: Formal meeting of witches that takes place on important dates, at major festivals, or sacred holidays that are celebrated on designated dates each year.

SALAMANDERS: Elemental of fire, ruled by Dijin.

SAMHAIN: Solemn festival, celebrated on October 31st by the Celts; it represented the death of the crops and the rest of the earth to create the new life in the winter.

SAMSARA: In Hindu philosophy, the endless wheel of life and death.

SELENE: In Greek mythology it is the Moon (*also called Artemis*), who travels the sky in search of her sleeping lover.

SHAMBALLAH: It has to do with the beliefs and culture of Tibet. According to the esoteric tradition, it is a purely etheric place, which is located in a reality parallel to ours and which is discovered when we develop our spiritual and mental part to unify ourselves with the energies of the cosmos.

SILFIDES: Elemental of the air, governed by Paralda.

SILFOS: Elemental of the air, governed by Paralda.

SOLSTICE: Time when the sun is in one of the two tropics, which occurs from June 21st to 22nd for the Cancer, and from December 21st to 22nd for the Capricorn. The first is that of summer in the northern hemisphere and that of winter in the southern hemisphere. The second is winter in the northern hemisphere and summer in the southern hemisphere.

SORTILEGE: It is any oracular system, to read luck. A spell is, the reading of luck.

SPELL: Witchcraft, enchantment ... Act by means of hypnotism, mental power, concoctions, etc., which allows a person versed in these issues mobilize entities and cosmic forces to get what you want.

TELEPATHY: It is included in the group of phenomena called PSE, Extrasensory Perception, it is called the paranormal faculty par excellence because there are few people who have not experienced it. Etymologically it means *"suffering at a distance"*. The definition given by Dr. J.B. Rhine: *"It is a communication of diverse impressions from one spirit to another, outside the sensory pathways."* At a general level it can be defined as: the unification of two nervous systems, separated by a space.

THEURGY: It is the equivalent of White Magic.

UNDINES: Elemental of water, ruled by Necna

WANING: It refers to the waning Moon phase, where it decreases.

WEST: It is the time lapse when the sun has already declined to be born again, between 6 in the afternoon and 12 at night.

WICCA: It is a kind of witchcraft, directly related to a religion, magical - naturalistic. This word, or Wicca are Anglo-Saxons of Celtic origin meaning *"The office of the wise"*, *"a person who knows"*.

WITCH: It is an English term meaning *"witch"*, from the same root of WIT (*ingenuity*) and WISE (*wise*).

WITCH CIRCLE: Normally, circles of protection, in the meadows are strange circles created by fungi, in ancient times were considered by religion as the place where spirits were invoked.

WITCHES' SABBATH: Castilian voice of SABBATH, comes from the Basque language AQUER or AKERRA = goat, and LARRE = meadow, that is, Goat Meadow. According to the legends this denomination is given to the Devil, because he presented himself to the assembly of witches and sorcerers in the form of a goat. The deformation of culture gave way to legends, at the beginning of Wicca in the attraction of similarities man disguised as reindeer to hunt, from there was born the story of the devil imposed by religion giving him the figure of a goat. The Witches' Sabbath is a meadow of the goats, meeting place of the Wicca festivities.

ZEPHYRS: Elemental of the air, governed by Paralda. They appear in the hours before midnight, are invoked with perfumes or fragrances of fresh flowers.

WICCA RITUALS SECRETS OF MAGIC AND WITCHCRAFT

In the lost universe of the magical knowledge of witches and magicians, mysterious beings of the Faeric world, WICCA the old religion is born, the adoration of nature, a hidden power, condemned and persecuted, full of strange phenomena and incredible portents, the world of MAGIC. The hidden forces of the great Sabbaths the power of the Esbats on moonlit nights, the liberation of the woman as a powerful mother, wise and witch. The preparation of old recipes that transform life, cure or sick, attract or remove, decrease and growth, the whole of the existence altered by magic.

The secret knowledge of sects, emperors, kings, businessmen, who sought in the magical secrets of witchcraft the power of triumph. After the time of darkness now the old religion is reborn, through this book is the door of the beginning of the path of the witch and the magician in the knowledge of mancias, the spell or reading of luck, secrets to transform the useless in the valuable, to know the natural cycle of the mutations and the changes of the seasons.

Discover the lunar force and its influence, open the doors of the parallel world of spirits and elementals, in this book is trapped the first letter of the path to initiation, who follow the steps of magic will undoubtedly find the power to create and transform destinations ... a magic book for magical people.

Universe of Magic
Encyclopedia

Do you want to learn magic?

Enter the school of magic through our Encyclopedia in Ophiuchus. The hidden power of the mind, the influence without space or time. A knowledge preserved for millenniums, now in your hands.